Snapshots of a Survivor

9 Days Affected by Childhood Sexual Trauma

Steven Shaw

KSH Books

Contents

Chapter One

Foreword

Since I began sharing my experiences many years ago, quite a few people have said to me, "You should write a book." This is one of the meanest things you could ever wish on someone. I tried. Over and over, I pulled out a notebook or opened a document on my laptop and attempted to find my way forward. The words would not flow in a way that seemed helpful. I was re-traumatized by the process. Paradoxically, the writing was simultaneously cathartic. I am still learning what healing looks like and how recovery from the deep wounds of trauma takes place. For me, part of the answer is found in disclosure and discussion. As painful as the telling of my story may be, being heard is validating. Being understood is satisfying. Being unconditionally loved is healing. You often find support when you are willing to be vulnerable.

More than a self-help book that regurgitates thoughts on childhood sexual trauma, I wanted to compose a narrative that would pull people into my world and help them see life from a survivor inside-out. I do not know if I have succeeded. Time will tell.

You will read about nine different days in my life affected by trauma. After you have spent some time in my shoes, I conclude with an epilogue that summarizes the rest of the story. Other parts may be added in the future, but for now, this suffices to give the reader a glimpse of a survivor's experience.

A dialog is further added that provides some exposition of the issue. Everything I share is stimulative, not exhaustive. Other books share greater technical insight into the way trauma affects the brain. Some focus on the emotional scars that form. Professional therapists and psychologists have put their expertise at our fingerprints in ways that dwarf the contribution of this brief volume.

My intent is to provide an accessible platform for furthering more discussion. Survivors need to know that they are not alone. Their experience, while unique, is not unusual. I want my fellow survivors to be able to find a safe space to speak up and to vocalize their suffering when ready. From experience, I know how harmful bearing the burden alone can be.

Sexual trauma is an especially dark attack on a person's soul. The violation is as intimate, spiritual and personal as can be experienced. A child's context for that abuse is limited. How do you interpret those circumstances? What damage does that inflict on your view of self? How does that affect your understanding of love and intimacy? I'm still learning.

Please know that the vivid descriptions of rape and sexual experience are not gratuitous. Without specifics, people can minimize the extent of the offense. If you are not angered, disgusted and overwhelmed, you do not understand what I faced. And my story is not among the worst.

"There is no greater agony than bearing an untold story inside you."

Maya Angelou

Chapter Two

Prologue

B e warned. You are about to engage with a graphic, disturbing and possibly triggering story. Based on true events, artistic license and conflation of events have been utilized to streamline the telling. Some names have been changed.

Chapter Three

Day 1

Skies had never been clearer in Ohio. An inverse ocean of pale blue stretched from horizon to horizon. Occasional wisps of cotton clouds passed over rolling, verdant hills. A state highway wound east from Pickerington, the black line meandering through a few small towns but mostly through fields of tasseled corn and heavy, ripening soybeans.

Near the village of Glenford sat a small house situated halfway down a broad hillside. Sitting back from the road, there appeared to be two stories from the front. In actual design, the home was a one-story ranch with a full basement that included a two-car garage. The upper story was sided vertically with dark brown planks. The lower was formed of concrete block painted white where visible. Like many Midwesterners, the family used one side of the garage for a vehicle and the other for storage. Extra vehicles sat in the lengthy driveway. If you turned into the lane that led to the garage doors, your car would stir the dust of the gravel on a hot, summer day like this. To your right, across the lawn, you would see a large garden sprouting with a few stalks of corn and rows of green beans, tomatoes, potatoes, onions, peas, zucchini, squash and strawberries. A few trees dotted the acreage.

On the rear corner of the house, mostly hidden from the drive was a tall Japanese elm. Extending above the roof, the limbs were easy to climb. Tucked on a branch nearly twelve feet above the ground was a boy. His dark hair was thick and tangled, longer on top than the sides and neatly trimmed around the ears and neck. His face was slightly freckled on his cheeks below his intense green eyes. His jeans were worn from many trips up and down the trunk. At the roots sat the other reason his clothes were dirty, a football. He was taking a break from his favorite pastime. Though the bright green leaves were thin, they were abundant and mostly blocked his view of the sky. He was not looking up anyway. His eyes were closed, and his imagination was running wild with thoughts of Ohio State football. He was planning his next game against another Big Ten rival. He was also avoiding a chore. By the time his father came home from the office, Kevin was supposed to have a row of strawberries weeded.

He had tried. With dirty tennis shoes on his small feet, he had trekked over to the shed and picked up a hoe. His eight-year-old frame was thin, slightly wider than the old tool. Down to the garden he went and viewed the task. Tendrils of strawberry plants ran wild for a few rows of the garden. They had been neatly planted originally, but strawberry fields tend towards chaos if not closely managed. These rows were chaotic indeed, out of character with the rest of the garden. Weeds sprung up in every little bit of earth uncovered by plants. Hoeing was going to be a limited option. He dropped to his knees and plucked a few large clumps of grass out of the ground. He discarded the waste with a toss onto the lawn.

Lawn was a generous term. The expanse of ground was mown field, grass mixed with native plants and an abundance of dandelions that had to be cut with an old lawn tractor weekly. Kevin wasn't quite big enough to manage that task just yet. For now, he was being given more responsibility with the push mower to cut the grass near the house. Driving the lawn tractor was something Kevin was looking forward to being able to do. Right now, the older teen guys in his church were the ones using it. They got to drive the tractor from his house down the state route to the church nearly a mile away. There, they mowed three acres of lawn before making the drive back to store the tractor in the garage.

Kevin's dad pastored the church. Nine years earlier, before Kevin was born, his mom and dad had moved to Glenford from Greenville, South Carolina for the purpose of establishing a new Baptist congregation. Dad was at the building now, studying in his office. Kevin stared at the twenty-five feet of berries stretched out ahead of him and looked for another large clump. If he could at least get those out, his dad would see that Kevin had made an attempt. He sighed. He had yet to play football today, and that's what he really wanted. He pulled some more grass and weeds from between the leaves. He saw a larger spot where the hoe might be helpful. Grasping the old wooden stick, he swung the tool over his shoulder and stepped through the plants to the space inhabited solely by weeds. He clawed at the earth with the rusty hoe getting to the roots like he had been instructed. He imitated the efforts he had observed in his father as best he could. Soon he had a small pile of debris. Scooping it up, he walked to the opposite side of the garden and tossed the arm load over the fence. That side was an untamed prairie. Once a year, the old farmer who owned that acreage would knock down the wild plants and thorn bushes with a brush hog. Frizzel was his last name. His mom attended the church Kevin's father pastored. In fact, she and her husband had donated the land for the large, brick structure that was now about three years old.

Back across the garden, Kevin looked at the amount of work he had accomplished. He acknowledged in his head that progress was minimal. His next sigh was louder and longer. He was beginning to wish he had gotten out of bed sooner. The cool hours of morning were gone. Noon heat was rising. It was too hot to weed. He could find the strength to play football but not to keep pulling these annoying plants. Should he walk back to the house and check the time? Maybe he could play one game before returning to his chore. Dad would not be home until 5:00. Kevin had some time. Up the hill to the house he trudged, a line of Canadian hemlock trees to his right. The row of fourteen-foot-tall, lithe trees helped define the boundaries of his football field. Other markers included a bird feeder, the elm tree he climbed, and two random maple trees his father had planted at opposite ends of the yard. He walked up the hill and reached the narrow plateau of backyard that then sloped to a small ridge before climbing more steeply to the crest of the hill and the neighbor's white ranch house. This patch of yard served as his stadium. He grabbed his football from the picnic table where he had left it the previous evening. Carrying it with him into the house, he set the ball on the lowest step and removed his shoes. He grabbed a glass and poured some sweet tea. His mom made the sweetest sun tea. The clock read 11:47. He had plenty of time.

"Are you done with the weeding?" Kevin's sister rounded the corner as she questioned him. Tiffany was nearly five years older and was making the transition from fun sibling to boring teenager. She no longer wanted to play outside. Kevin resented the question. She was not his boss.

"No. But I got plenty of time." He paused. "You could help me." He looked at her hopefully.

"I have my own chores."

At least yours are inside, he thought.

"And I have to practice piano," she added.

She practiced a lot. And she was getting pretty good. "Yeah. Must be nice to be inside all day. It's getting hot out there." He couldn't resist.

"If you had gotten busy earlier, you'd be done by now."

You couldn't win with this one.

He shrugged. "I was tired. You weren't up that early either."

Kevin's room was in the basement. Forty percent of the space was garage. A strip of hallway ran from the stairs connecting the two floors to the open space which was divided between the laundry and play area and Kevin's bedroom. A small half bathroom had been built just inside the open space on the left wall before you got to the laundry area. Kevin kept his limited hygiene products in the mirrored medicine cabinet. For an eight-year-old, the contents of the cabinet were minimal: deodorant he sometimes forgot to apply, a toothbrush, toothpaste, a comb and a bottle of Canoe cologne that was used less frequently than the deodorant. The downstairs space was unfinished. The joists supporting the first floor were open. His sister's room was directly above his. He could hear when she was walking around. She liked to laze around in bed in the morning, too.

"I'm just saying, you could have been out there when it was cooler."

He had no argument for that. So, he gulped his tea, put his shoes on, grabbed the football and headed back outside.

As he walked along the back of the house, he heard the kitchen window rise. His sister called out, "I'm making a sandwich for lunch in a few minutes. Want me to make one for you?"

She could be pretty nice. "Sure. I want peanut butter and jelly."

"Okay." He turned away. "Hey! One more thing." He turned back to the window and was met with a stream of cold water. She was spraying him with the sink hose through the screen. And laughing. She was really laughing hard.

"Hey!" Kevin yelled and ran out of reach.

"Are you still hot?" she asked.

"You owe me two sandwiches." Kevin wiped the water from his face. "I'll be back in a little bit."

Tossing the football into the air and catching it with his hands, he made his way back to the garden. He surveyed the strawberry field as if he had not just been there. A longer sigh escaped his lips. This time he decided to clear a small area before going back to the house for lunch. With his shirt still a bit damp, he really didn't mind his sister's prank. He was slightly disgusted that he didn't see it coming. After all, he had seen his parents pull this trick a few times.

He would get even with her. Caution was required. He could easily get in trouble. Boys had to be really polite to girls, especially their sisters. His parents had beat that into him, sometimes literally.

Marking out a roughly five by three foot area, he determined to rid that space of every single weed before eating lunch. Once he made up his mind, he made quick progress. The hoe was too unwieldy for tight spaces. He was reduced to using his hands. Getting on his knees, he pulled weed after weed tossing them into the field to be mown under later. His dad would see all the weeds Kevin had pulled. Throwing that bunch over the fence into the neighboring field had been foolish. He needed Dad to see evidence of his hard work. Minutes passed as he grasped and pulled, grasped and pulled. Progress was gradually becoming noticeable. He began to lightly sweat. Maybe he should ask his sister to spray him again. As he finished clearing the small square of space, his stomach growled.

"Time for a sandwich," he thought. "And more tea."

Standing up, he dusted off the knees of his pants. Picking the football from the turf, ran up the hill, the ball stuck in the crook of his right elbow as he imagined himself running through the Wolverine defense.

He crossed the back of the house, eyeing the window to make sure his sister wasn't ready to strike again. Stepping on the deck attached to the side of the house nearest the highway, he tromped across the aged two-by-fours darkly stained to match the siding. He set the football on the deck, opened the white screen door of the main entrance, and bounced up the two steps to the main level, worn red carpet under his feet. Then he backed himself right back down, slipped his shoes off and restarted his journey to the kitchen. At the top of the steps he could see into the dining room and kitchen on the left and the living room on the right. Tiffany was at the piano against the far wall of the living room. Her hands were running back and forth performing a skilled exercise. He ignored her and walked through the small dining room into the kitchen. Two peanut butter and jelly sandwiches sat on the counter. He refilled his glass and moved his food to the table. His sister was still repeating the same exercise over and over. With each repetition she attempted to move her fingers a bit quicker.

"Hey!" Kevin yelled. "Can't you play a real song?"

It was her turn to ignore him. But she only repeated the exercise a few more times before stopping and entering the dining room. She sat at the table with him. He was already on the second sandwich.

"Thanks for the grub. I didn't think you knew the recipe," he teased.

Tiffany rolled her eyes. "Yeah, it's a tough one. Too bad I can't follow a recipe and make cookies."

"Mmm. You should try anyway. No-bakes would be good."

"You're kidding, right? I am never making no-bakes with you again. Ever."

They both laughed. A few weeks earlier, Kevin had begged his mom to make the delicious peanut butter and chocolate no-bake cookies after dinner.

"I've had a long day. You can make them yourself."

"Aw, Mom. I've never made them before. I don't know how." Sometimes, he thought his mother had never been his age. She seemed to think he was a miniature adult.

"Tiffany, help your brother."

Tiffany shot Kevin a look that would have killed him, if possible, a look that said, "I had other plans for the evening." She did not dare protest her mother in this mood though. Mom headed off to her bedroom.

Tiffany decided to get through this as quickly as possible. She rushed to the stove and turned the front burner to medium heat. Once she knew Mom was out of earshot, she turned back to Kevin. "You really can't make these by yourself?" She was annoyed.

"I can next time. But I've never done it alone before. I didn't know she was going to make you help me. But, come on, it won't take long, and they're so good." He smiled at her. "You want some, too. I know you do."

She lightened up slightly. He could sense it. He was getting better at diffusing tension with humor. He was learning that if you could make people laugh, they would be less likely to be mad at you.

Tiffany reached up and opened the cupboard. She grabbed the Tupperware container that held the sugar and lowered it to the stove. She couldn't resist a final word.

"Next time, ask me before you ask Mom." She turned back to scoop out the sugar and made a startling realization. She had set the Tupperware on the hot eye. Quickly she grabbed the container to remove it. As she lifted the box off the stovetop, streams of melted plastic strung out from the bottom, and the sugar poured out of the now-ruined box onto the stove. Odors of burning sugar and melting plastic filled the air. She set the container down and turned off the burner.

Tiffany looked at Kevin, a mix of horror and hysteria on her face. She wanted to laugh at the absurdity of her mistake, but she also knew that Mom would be livid.

The world paused as the two siblings stared at each other.

Tiffany took a deep breath. "Go tell Mom." Her voice echoed the resignation she felt to the core of her soul. Mom would not take this well. This tragedy was layered. Mom's rest would be interrupted. Tupperware was not cheap. And the sugar would be largely wasted. Plus, there was the mess to be cleaned up. Mom did not like messes. Dad did not either. "We may be poor," they would say, "but we are clean."

"I'm not telling her," Kevin shot back. "You did it."

As if her spirit departed her body, Tiffany slumped. Resigning herself to fate and committing her life to God, she headed down the short hallway to the door at the end. Behind that closed door was her parents' bedroom.

The next ten minutes were a blur of frustration and anger. Then Mom shouted a few final instructions and stormed back to her room.

Tiffany and Kevin finished cleaning up the mess together and then made the cookies. Something good had to come out of this after all.

"Yeah. I'm okay with that," pondered Kevin at the thought. "What about chocolate chip?"

"What about waiting for dinner? We're going to the Parks. You know Mrs. Kathy will have dessert."

"The Parks?!" Kevin was excited. Art and Kathy Parks were members of the church in Glenford and lived out in the country about twenty minutes away. Their farm was a 40 plus acre property at the end of a long, gravel lane much longer than their own driveway. Their children were teenagers. Sam was seventeen. Kara was fifteen. Kara and Kevin's sister, Tiffany, were good friends and getting closer.

Kevin idolized Sam. He was cool. His car was a gold Trans Am. He had tons of stuff Kevin hoped to have someday. He even had a personal computer. This was a huge deal in the 1980s. Kevin could play the Microsoft Flight Simulator, and Sam also had a football game. Playing those programs was a rush of euphoria for Kevin.

With bright eyes, Kevin exclaimed, "Maybe I can play on the computer!"

"Are you going to cry this time if Sam puts on the mask?"

She could be a real buzzkill. The last time they had been at the Park's past dark, they played hide and go seek. Sam put on a frightening monster mask. Kevin was not expecting this, and when he peaked out from behind a couch to find a monster in his face, he reacted the only sane way any child would – he screamed and ducked back behind the couch again. Sam thought this was hilarious, as did Kara and Tiffany. Kevin's crying also attracted the attention of the adults. When they uncovered the reason for Kevin's tears, they also found the situation to be humorous. Sam, however, was admonished not to do it again.

"I won't be scared this time," Kevin vowed. "I just didn't know who it was."

"Sure," she agreed, but the sarcasm was undeniable.

With that memory overshadowing his day, Kevin slipped into his tennis shoes, burled through the door, and grabbed his football. The clock now read 1:12. He had time to play a little football and to finish his chore. Football first.

Jim Karsatos hunched under center. "Hike!" he yelled and turned to hand the ball to Keith Byars. Scampering to the sideline, Byars was pushed out of bounds by a Michigan defender but too late to stop the first down. Karsatos under center again. "Hike!" He turned and faked another handoff to Byars. This time he rolled out and threw a deep, high ball to Chris Carter. The ball was nearly out of reach, but Carter dove and got his fingers underneath the ball as he hit the ground. A catch! First and goal. Karsatos was on fire. "Hike!" This time he threw a quick fade to Carter. Touchdown! Ohio State was up big on their rival now.

Kevin slipped out of his fantasy and jogged over to the elm. Dropping the football, he jumped to grab a small piece of rope he had tied up in the tree. With a loop at the end, he could use it to pull himself up even after Dad lopped off the lower branches to make mowing easier. From the rope, he latched on to a branch and pulled himself higher into the canopy. Once there, he situated himself and allowed his mind to wander back to football. He wanted to play wide receiver. That feeling when the ball seems just out of reach but you can grasp it with your fingers and make the catch was a feeling he wanted to chase the rest of his life. His little Christian school did not have a football team. However, the local high school, Sheridan, had a great football program. A few teenagers in his church attended Sheridan. Maybe his parents would let him switch schools when he got bigger. The minutes lapsed as his mind wandered.

He had sat in the tree long enough. Time to get back to his chore. He lowered himself to a branch and jumped out of the tree rolling in the grass as he landed. Tumbling was fun. Grabbing the football, he took off down the hill. One last pass to himself as he neared the garden. Another fantastic catch. At the edge of the garden, he looked down the row. What seemed like major progress now looked futile. Had weeds grown back during lunch? It certainly seemed so. Still, there were all the dead plants strewn in the grass. He had done something. He needed to do more, or he might get a spanking. Marking out a small area to conquer seemed to make the most sense. Bit by bit he would get this row of strawberries under control. Back to work, he got into a rhythm of pulling and piling. When he finally got a decent pile, he would carry it to the garden boundary and dump it in the grass. He liked it better when his dad worked with him, or his sister. But that was rare. His dad put the bulk of his effort into planting the garden, painstakingly laying out the rows after tilling. Occasionally, after the earth had been churned, Kevin would find an arrowhead or random piece of flint. His father found a lot more.

Dad would say, "We're going to have 3 rows of green beans, 3 rows of potatoes, a row of onions, a row of peas, 2 rows of tomatoes, three hills of zucchini, 3 hills of yellow squash and a row of corn." Interestingly, corn did not do that well. The soil was not quite right. Once the garden was planted, Dad would slip down to the garden in the early hours of the day and water, if necessary. He would also till the rows. Kevin was required to do some of the maintenance. Mom would help with harvesting. Kevin and Tiffany were often tasked with snapping beans or shelling peas. Mom and Dad would can vegetables and store them in the garage. Kevin didn't really care for vegetables, especially when Mom threw a bunch of them in tomato broth for soup. He had probably received more spankings for refusing to eat vegetable soup than for any other offense except fighting with Chuck at church.

Another small patch was cleared of big weeds. He began to focus on the most noticeable clumps. After all, he wanted maximum visual impact for Dad to see. While he worked, he daydreamed. And the afternoon slipped by.

"Kevin!" His sister's yell interrupted his peaceful labor. "Kevin!" She was screaming from her open bedroom window.

"What?!" He shouted back.

"Mom called. She said to tell you to come in and get ready to go. You need a bath."

Yes, he did. His hands were dusty, and his clothes were grass-stained from his strenuous efforts on the football field.

"Okay. I'm coming."

She was smart to tell him that Mom was the one ordering the plan of events. He only listened to his sister when she was echoing Mom or Dad. After all, she was not his boss. She was barely bigger than he was. They used to play together all the time, as equals. Now that she was a teenager, she acted like she outranked him. He could be the boss, too. If she could, he could. He didn't think that telling others what to do was so difficult – try actually doing the work, like the weeding he had accomplished today! That was hard. He surveyed the row of strawberries one last time. He wasn't sure he had technically completed his father's wish. Maybe not all of the weeds were removed, but progress was visible. He thought Dad would be okay with it.

He scooped up the football, tucked the leather under his elbow and ran up the hill. Instead of making his way behind the house, he jogged across the gravel driveway to the garage. The doors for the vehicles were closed, but the side door was unlocked. As he stepped inside, he felt the cool air. He had not initially enjoyed the move to the basement. Before his little sister, Agnes, was born, he had a small bedroom upstairs. The simple layout of the ranch put him across the narrow hall from the bathroom. His greatest fear was awaking in the middle of the night and needing to pee. To get to the bathroom, he had to cross three feet of hallway. While that does not seem so threatening, at the far end of the hallway was the main door. He was never quite sure that something was not out there looking in at him. Having a vivid imagination is fantastic when you dream of football but not so great when you look down the hallway to that portal to the vast beyond. The world was huge out there. Fortunately, to his right was the door to his sister's room and then the next door at the end of the hall was his parents' bedroom. So, stoked by the courage that comes from knowing your friends are closer than your enemies, he would leap across the hallway, quickly shut the door and enjoy the safety of the bathroom.

Then Agnes came along. His dad explained that options were limited. Kevin could share a room with a baby, or he could move to the basement. Papa and Dad built in a wall and closet to separate the newly created bedroom from the reduced play area and laundry room. They also installed a wood-burning furnace and chimney on that end of the house. Carpeted with remnants from who knows where, burnt orange carpet flecked with brown covered the concrete floor. Papa had thought to lay down a thick pad first. A bed was set up with a bedside stand. A bookshelf and a desk and a chest of drawers completed the furnishings. Mom made a valance curtain to hang over the tiny window that sat at ground level. The two outside walls were concrete. Dad painted the walls yellow. Mom covered the bed with a deep green, Navajo-patterned comforter. Kevin was skeptical. On the one hand, this would be his personal space, and the room was much larger than his original bedroom. But this was the basement. The bedroom window upstairs was far above the ground where monsters could not see. But this window was low enough for any sized creep. Now, to get to the bathroom, he would have to cross an entire room, naked to whatever horrors peered through those window wells.

His first night downstairs could not have been worse. Dad tucked him into bed, said a prayer and turned out the light, shutting the door behind him. Kevin lay under the covers looking at the window directly over his head. The night seemed calm. Whatever monsters might be out there, they were ignoring him for now. A lamp occupied the bedside table. Would turning it on help? He decided against it.

Visibility would only help the bad guys. Instead, he covered himself and fell asleep with a corner of the comforter over his head. In the middle of the night, he awakened. All was still. Nevertheless, he was overcome with fear and ran upstairs to his parents' room. Then he faced another conundrum. Should he go in? He was afraid on all accounts – scared to go back to the dungeon and frightened of getting in trouble for walking into his parents' room. He looked back down the hallway and imagined the evil beings staring at him from outside. He chose his lesser fear and quietly slipped inside. A small room with closet doors on the wall to his left, the headboard was against the opposite wall. Nearest to him were his parents' feet. Should he wake them? No. That could go poorly indeed. He got down on his knees and crawled between the foot of the bed and the closet doors to the outside wall. Windows would have allowed him to see his climbing tree if the curtains were open. They were not. He curled up on the floor. Dad was on that side of the bed. Kevin felt safe. He fell asleep. A short time later, Dad stirred, needing to use the bathroom. He looked at the clock. Just past 1:00 AM. He had time to get back to sleep. As he sat up and rolled his legs over the edge of the bed to stand, he noticed the diminutive body in a ball.

"Kevin," he whispered. No response. The kid was out cold. Dad touched his arm, and Kevin stirred. "Kevin, what are you doing?"

The little boy murmured, "I was scared."

Dad muttered, "Of course" under his breath. He was not surprised. "Go back to your room. There's no reason to be scared. We prayed. Jesus will take care of you."

Dad got out of bed and headed to the bathroom. Kevin followed as far as the bathroom door.

"Keep going," Dad added. "It's okay."

Emboldened by the knowledge that Dad was awake if anything went awry, Kevin padded down the hallway, tepidly stepped down the two stairs to the landing in front of the main door, quickly scurried past the door looking back at the light from the bathroom and stepped down the stairs toward the basement. A second landing made for a comfortable turn before the last two stairs led into the basement hallway. Kevin could go no further. The basement was too dark, the hallway too long, his bed too distant. In fear, he huddled on the landing. Still half asleep from his nap next to Dad's bed, he went back to sleep. His small body occupied roughly half of the landing. He was just a little boy after all.

His mom discovered him in the morning.

"Kevin, what are you doing? Why are you sleeping here? Why aren't you in your bed?"

He was confused.

"I was scared," he admitted.

"There's nothing to be afraid of," Mom offered. Parents really know how to make everything okay, Kevin thought. Little did they know.

He got the sense that he was in the way, so he got up and stumbled to his room, climbed back in bed and tried to resume his sleep.

The nights after that got easier. He had a little night light in his room and one in the bathroom. He became comfortable navigating between those two beacons in the wee hours of the morning when necessary. He liked having his personal space. His shelves slowly filled with books. He started a collection of figurine dogs. Most of them were smaller than the palm of his hand. Dad nailed a small memento shelf next to the doorway. Mom and Dad added a Nerf basketball hoop above the door. With the ceiling unfinished, there was additional space for shooting the ball. He now had a room like his sister, Tiffany.

Like her, he could shut the door and be alone. He rarely needed to take that step. He was mostly alone regardless.

Today, he was especially grateful for the cool downstairs' temperatures. Crossing the garage, he went through the door into the adjoining basement. He turned right down the hallway toward his room, entering only long enough to grab clean clothes before heading upstairs for a bath.

As a pastor's family, providing and receiving hospitality was not unusual. For Kevin, those events were always exciting. He especially liked going to other people's homes. When company came to the Stephens' house, sometimes he had extra chores like helping with dishes, cleaning and even giving up his room to overnight guests. When Mom used her special china, she preferred that Dad and Tiffany do the washing and drying. He was tasked with Tupperware and Correlle dishes.

Going to the Park's was especially fun. Mrs. Kathy was a good cook. Food was a major factor in determining which families Kevin wanted to visit. Another factor was having kids around his age. That was not the case with the Parks. But Sam allowed Kevin to hang out in his room, so at least he had a playmate. Sometimes Kevin wanted a brother, especially when he had to work in the garden. He needed someone to boss around like Tiffany did to him.

Kevin could hear the house come to life as Mom, baby sister and Dad all came home to prepare for the evening.

"Hurry up!" yelled Mom as she walked past the door. That was not an unusual command. Kevin enjoyed playing in the bathtub. Given the freedom, he would play for an hour. Especially fun was plugging the drain, turning on the shower and pretending to be in a sinking submarine. He finished his bath, pulled the drain on the tub and grabbed a worn blue towel. He dressed in a fresh set of jeans, a striped t-shirt and socks. He hung up his towel neatly. When he left the bathroom, everything was arranged as if he had never used it. He took a last look, approved and turned off the light. He carried his dirty laundry downstairs and used the hamper next to the washer. He put on his shoes. He was ready to go. Dad came down the stairs.

"Did you finish weeding a row of strawberries?"

Kevin shuffled his feet and avoided eye contact. "I think so."

"You think so? Either you did or you didn't."

"I got most of them. Did you see?"

"I haven't been down there yet, and there's no time now. I'll look at it tomorrow, so if you need to do a little more work, you should get that done before supper."

Kevin let out a sigh of relief. He didn't think he had done too badly, but at least he was in no danger of a spanking tonight.

"Yes, sir."

His dad touched his shoulder. "I'm proud of you for working on it today. That's a big help."

Kevin looked his father in the eyes. Dad seemed to be proud of him.

"Did you put the hoe away?" Dad asked.

"Oh, shoot."

"Go throw it in the shed and then get in the car. We're about to leave."

Kevin dashed out of the house and down to the garden. He grabbed the old tool and carried it to the shed. Sliding the white tin door back, he put the hoe against the wall with other implements. He shut the door and started back to the driveway. Turning back to the garden, he took one last look at the strawberries. The row looked a lot better. And he would finish whatever weeds were left tomorrow, early, before the day got so hot.

When he got in the back seat, Tiffany was already there. She was a tough act to follow. As much as he liked to tease her, he admired his older sister. Her grades were exceptional. She rarely got in trouble. She was sweet with him most of the time. They had more fun when she was younger, but life was changing. A baby sister had altered dynamics as well. Everyone pitched in to help in one way or another. If nothing else, more independence was required of the two older children. And here they sat, in the back seat of a red Ford Granada. Mom, Agnes in her arms, and Dad exited from the upstairs door. They walked down the outside stairs from the deck to the driveway. Dad locked the garage entrance. Mom stuck Agnes in the back seat. Tiffany and Kevin adjusted accordingly, sliding towards the opposite door. Kevin thought about picking a little fight over space but thought better of it when he saw the serious look on Mom's face. This was not the time. Dad climbed in and started the car. He backed into the turnaround space and headed out the gravel drive towards the highway. He paused and waited to see if any traffic would pop over the hill to the right. Vision to the left was excellent. You could see the church building nearly a mile away from here. But that hill could cause problems. He accelerated out of the driveway and got up to 55 as quickly as the old Granada would allow. This car wasn't so bad, thought Kevin. He liked the power windows.

Down the road they cruised, passing the Frizzell property which encompassed almost all the property on the left-hand side from the Stephens' house to the church. Then they passed the Cooperrider farm. Their 2-story farmhouse sat close to the road on the right side of the highway, the white clapboarding in need of a fresh coat of paint. Before reaching the church, Dad turned right off the state route on to a short lane that cut over to a country road. The gravel kicked up behind them and dust rose skyward. Dad stopped. He turned right again on to the tar and gravel surface of Hopewell Indian Road. He drove east until he turned left and headed north. Staring out the window, Kevin thought about playing with Sam. The last couple of times he had been in Sam's room, Sam had shut the door and shown him some catalogs. He was particularly enthralled with a section where women's clothes were advertised. And he liked the pages that showed the women in their underwear. Kevin liked them too. They were pretty. He wondered if Sam would show him some more pictures tonight.

"Everyone be on their best behavior," he caught Mom saying as he tuned back into life inside the car. He had heard this lecture many times. "Whatever Mrs. Kathy serves, you need to eat, even if it's vegetable soup," she added specifically for Kevin's benefit. "Don't forget to ask to be excused from the table when dinner is over. And don't break anything." That was more for Tiffany. She was the one who was accident prone.

One more lefthand turn off of the roughly paved road onto a gravel lane. Back through some woods and over some small hills with scattered houses along the way, they drove until they nearly reached the end. The Parks owned both houses that were visible from their driveway. Down the lane just a bit further was a two-story farmhouse much like the Cooperrider's, but this one was fern green. The family that lived there rented from Sam's dad. Their family name was Hamilton, and one of the kids had been Kevin's classmate at the Christian school since kindergarten. His name was Joshua. He had ten siblings and one of them was Tiffany's classmate since kindergarten, too. Surprisingly, no one was outside. All thirteen members of the Hamilton clan must be inside at dinner. Kevin could only imagine how chaotic life would be with that many kids.

The Park's home was slightly up the hill at the edge of a large wood. Their acreage also included fields some of which were used for hay.

A small pond was at the bottom of the drive. Inevitably, ducks were swimming on the surface or nesting to the side. Dad stopped the car just past the pond near the top of the drive. The house was a couple of stories, much wider than it was tall. The ground floor was garage and recreational space. Upstairs were the kitchen, dining room and bedrooms. A large glass window allowed a view of the pond from the upstairs sitting room.

Kevin had spent lots of time here. Sometimes, Mrs. Kathy was his babysitter before he was old enough to attend school or at times during the summers since. She was a lady. Although she was funny and pleasant, she conducted herself in a way that evinced sophistication. Art was easygoing and goofy. He loved to laugh. He was a banker, the president of a bank, in fact. Kathy stayed at home. Both of them came from money, to some degree. Kevin didn't know the details. He just knew they had nice stuff. They could afford things that most of the people he knew could not. Dad had done some work for Art. He painted the bank building in downtown Newark where Art was president. Kevin tagged along a time or two. He wasn't much help, but he was with Dad. He liked that. And Mom liked the peace and quiet. Kevin could get chatty, real talkative. But for now, Kevin was calm. The long day of weeding had reduced his energy. The young family stepped onto the porch and knocked at the lower door. Greeted by Kathy, they were welcomed up the stairs and into the dining room.

"We're ready to eat," said Kathy as she set the last dish of food on the table. Art and Sam stepped in. Kara had already found Tiffany, and they were seated. The rest found a seat, and Art asked Dad to pray over the food. Dad was always asked to pray when they went anywhere. Kevin sometimes led the prayer at home, or Tiffany or Mom. But Dad prayed a lot. Kevin hoped Dad would keep the prayer short. Kevin was starving. Dad said amen after a mercifully short utterance of thanks to

God. Mrs. Kathy began uncovering the dishes and serving the food. The main dish was ham. This was going to be a simple, Midwestern, meat-and-potatoes kind of meal. Dad preferred Mrs. Kathy's chop suey but today was simple fare. She uncovered some cheesy carrots with crackers crumbled on top.

"I also have macaroni and cheese," she stated.

Kevin was excited. Macaroni and cheese was delicious. She removed the lid. Kevin's eyes went wide and his face could not hide his disappointment...and disgust. The macaroni and cheese was green. The Parks started laughing.

"Sam thought it would be funny to add food dye to the macaroni," explained Art.

Mom and Dad began to laugh. Tiffany giggled. Kevin did not look pleased. He was upset. This did not look edible. And he knew his mom would insist on making him eat. She always insisted. "You never know where God is going to call you to be a missionary. You may have to eat things you don't like. This is good practice." He had heard that speech many times.

As plates were filled with food, Kevin handed his dish to Mrs. Kathy. He crossed his fingers that she would allow him some latitude on menu selection. She asked for his approval as she placed ham on his plate. He nodded. Then she received his approval for cheesy carrots and green beans with bacon. Then she got to the macaroni. "Would you like some mac 'n cheese?"

Kevin glanced at his mother. She was busy with the baby. He shook his head no. She smiled. "Are you sure? It doesn't change the flavor just the color." Again, he glanced at Mom. Still busy. He shook his head. "No, thank you," he whispered as loud as Mrs. Kathy could hear and as low as Mom could not. "Okay," she said. "If you change your mind, you can try some later." She handed him the plate. His countenance expressed relief. Kathy couldn't help but laugh at his confusion. "Sam is such a prankster." Kevin looked at Sam, and he was staring back with a smile. He took a forkful of macaroni and opened widely. "Mmm," he moaned as he ate. "This is so good."

Kevin did not believe him. How could something that looked so disgusting taste good? Sam could eat all of it.

Fortunately, the rest of the meal was delicious and satisfying. Kevin finished his food and asked for more cheesy carrots. Then he looked around, searching for evidence of a dessert. Kathy knew him well.

"Ready for some chocolate?" she asked. She already knew the answer. Everyone knew the answer. Kevin loved chocolate. He was a pretty smart child, precocious and curious. But some concepts gave him difficulty. One word that troubled him was "allergies." He really didn't understand what that meant. Tiffany loved horses, and she was allergic to them. Over time, Kevin conflated liking something with being allergic to it. Then he was asked point blank by Mrs. Kathy one time, "Do you have any allergies?" Kevin's response was, "I am allergic to turtles and chocolate." She had been confused by the answer. "I thought you liked chocolate."

"Oh, I love chocolate. I am allergic to it."

Kathy had called Mom. "Is Kevin allergic to chocolate?"

"Not at all," Mom replied. "It's all he ever wants!"

"That's what I thought. But he told me he's allergic."

Thankfully, the misunderstanding was worked out. But the teasing started immediately. Kevin knew it was coming now.

"Oh," said Art, "Keverino can't have chocolate. He's allergic. I'll take his dessert."

Everyone laughed. Kevin chuckled nervously. "I'm over it," he announced. "I am no longer allergic."

"Still," Sam added, "We should probably err on the safe side. We don't want you to swell up like a pig."

Kevin bowed his head slightly in contrition. He would never live this down.

Mrs. Kathy served him a big square of brownie and added some vanilla ice cream on the side. He could always count on her to be nice even if Art and Sam gave him a hard time.

Now his little belly was full. He wasn't sure he could move.

"Time to go play," said Mom. "The adults are going to talk for a while. Kevin, you can go with Sam."

Sam laughed. He stood up. He was a tall young man, seventeen years of age and rail thin. He didn't play sports, even though he looked athletic. He preferred hunting and fishing. "Let's go, boy!" And down the hall they went.

Kevin walked into Sam's bedroom. The Park's home had its own scent. He had noticed this as he had spent time in the various houses of parishioners. He had no names for these aromas. But if you had blindfolded him and placed him in a home, he could have identified at least a few with no hesitation: Wisemans, Scalfs, Wests, Daniels and Parks. His own home seemed to have no smell. He wondered if that was because he was used to it, or if it was just neutral. Some homes had almost no scent at all. But some were pungent. And Kevin had grown familiar with these aromas and found them comforting.

Sam had a bunk bed. Kevin loved bunk beds. He enjoyed the lower bunk and the sense of being in a room within a room. The bed was disheveled, the navy sheets and comforter still askew from the previous night. Kevin was not allowed to leave his room without first making his bed. Holding back his urge to fold the coverings, he settled on the floor. Sam closed the door.

"I want to show you something." Sam opened his closet and searched. Out came the catalog. He sat down on the floor beside Kevin. Flipping through the pages, he found the section he wanted. There were the women in undergarments. Kevin was intrigued. His underwear was so simple. Women were hiding all of these straps and extra pieces of cloth under their clothes? What were those pieces of cloth covering? He had observed his baby sister nursing on Mom's breasts. He kind of understood what was happening there. But that other sliver of cloth, similar to what he wore in some cases, what was that covering?

Sam was flipping page by page through pictures of bras, thongs, hi-cuts, bikinis and lingerie.

"Have you ever touched a penis?" Sam asked.

Kevin shook his head.

"Not even your own? How do you take a bath?" Sam laughed.

Kevin looked at him. "Yeah, I guess I touch my own penis when I'm in the bathtub."

"Look at mine." Sam unzipped his jeans and pulled them down over his butt. Then he exposed his aroused penis. He stroked it. "You can touch it."

Kevin was nervous. He had never touched anyone else's private place. He had kissed Stacy Hocken when he was in first grade. She liked it. And he held Kristina's hand during nap time in kindergarten. But he had never thought about touching a guy. That was weird. Guys didn't kiss and touch each other like a guy touches a girl.

He looked at Sam. He liked having Sam's approval. When he was at church, and the older kids let him be in their group but denied the other kids, Kevin felt special. He thought it was partly because he was the preacher's kid. But he thought they liked him, too. He made them laugh sometimes. And he spoke more like a grown-up than a child. He had started reading at the age of 3 and had read more books than most teenagers. He felt like a grown-up in some ways. Now he was doing something very grown-up.

He reached out and touched the penis. Something was dripping from the tip. Just like his penis, there was a slit in the tip where pee could come out. But this wasn't pee. He did not want to look stupid, so he did not ask any questions. This was something he had learned, too. If you let people talk, you could usually figure out what was going on without looking like an idiot.

Sam groaned. "That feels good. You can touch all of it. Use both hands."

Kevin moved slowly, unsurely. He grabbed the penis just like he observed Sam doing and moved his hands around. The wetness was getting on his fingers and palms. Sam took some and licked it off his fingers. "It doesn't taste like anything. You can lick it right off."

He guided Kevin's head toward his crotch. Thoughts swirled through Kevin's head but mostly he wanted Sam to like him. He moved closer, closed his eyes and touched the penis with his lips. Sam moaned again.

"Let me see your penis," said Sam.

Kevin was uncomfortable. He did everything in private. Because he had an older sister, he always had to change behind closed doors. He stood up and pulled his pants down. Sam reached up and helped him with his underwear. Sam touched him. Kevin felt the sensation. It felt good.

"Lay down with me," Sam suggested.

Kevin laid down parallel with the young man, his back to him. He felt the rigid member between his legs sliding back and forth. The thrusting started just above his knees, but he could feel Sam working his way up his legs towards his butt. Sam's penis made contact with

Kevin's butthole. The penetration was light but forceful. Then he pushed a bit harder and deeper. Kevin felt discomfort and grunted. Sam pulled him back over to face him.

"I want you to put your mouth on my penis again. That felt good."

Kevin acquiesced. This time something else came from Sam's penis as he masturbated near Kevin's lips. Cream spilled out. Some shot across Sam's body. Sam lay there panting. Kevin observed all of this and felt his own penis. Sam reached out and touched him, too.

"Feels good, doesn't it?"

Kevin nodded.

"Want to play on the computer?" Sam asked. "Or would you rather play pinball?"

The Parks had an arcade style pinball machine downstairs.

"I want to see how far I can fly the plane."

"Flight Simulator it is." Sam pulled off a tubed sock and used it to clean himself off. His penis was already getting hard again. He leaned back for a moment and used the sock to stiffen himself further. Then he threw the sock towards a hamper, stood up and pulled his underwear and jeans back up.

The whole episode lasted about fifteen to twenty minutes while the adults were at the table down the hall and while the sisters were talking in the room next door. Everyone was close and yet a world away. Sam opened the door. The computer sat in an open workspace adjacent to the stairs. Sam pushed a button. Kevin heard a whir, and the unit slowly came to life. Kevin and Sam sat side by side controlling the simulator. Sam explained more of how the game worked and then gave Kevin opportunities to try. Too soon for Kevin's liking, Mom and Dad sounded the departure warning.

"Thanks for letting Kevin play on the computer, Sam." Dad shook Sam's hand.

Sam put his other hand on Kevin's head. "He's a lot of fun. Send him over any time."

Goodbyes were said, and the family headed back to the Granada for the short drive home.

"Did you have a good time tonight?" asked Dad as he tucked Kevin into bed that night.

"Yes, sir. Can we get a computer like that?"

"Probably not, son. I think those are a little too expensive. You don't need a computer yet anyway. Maybe when you get a little older. Good night, Kevin. I love you."

"I love you, Daddy."

Dad stepped out of the bedroom, shutting the overhead light off as he did so. He shut the door behind him. Kevin heard the soft click of the latch. In the darkness, he was alone. His thoughts repeated the events in Sam's bedroom. He could not turn them off as he drifted into sleep.

Chapter Four

Day 2

Weeks passed. Summer turned into fall. Kevin loved autumn. Even though he had to return to school, he didn't mind so much because football season was about to start. As the daylight gradually decreased, the leaves turned and the temperatures cooled, each day brought him closer to his birthday in November. This would be his ninth. He was *not* thrilled to be nine years old. He *was* enthusiastic about being another year closer to a teenager and an adult. Grownups had all the freedom. They didn't do the things they did not want to do, he thought. All the people he looked up to in life were adults. He could not wait to join the club.

But November was several weeks off. Summer was waning but still the season. School had started, and he was anticipating every Saturday like a national holiday. This particular Saturday was as perfect a day as you could expect in Ohio in late September. Sunshine was completely off the dimmer. Kevin was still in bed when the sun crested the eastern hills. Dad was not. He was in the garden, alone, just like the old hymn says. He was not singing though. No one could have heard him if he was. He was steering a tiller down the rows burying the remnants under the soil to lay dormant over the winter. The plants would decay back into the earth out of which they had sprung creating richer soil for the following year.

The garden had yielded its bounty. Just enough rain had fallen that additional watering had been mostly unnecessary. Yes, Dad had run the hose from the house to the garden a few times but not as often as previous years. Harvest was complete. Beans had been picked and snapped by the bushel. Many of them now sat in Mason jars on the shelves in the garage. Onions had been chopped up for salads and cooked on the stove with liver. Zucchini had been baked into loaves of bread, given away at church, dropped on people's porches, and left in cars that were unlocked and unattended. The yellow squash had been sauteed with the onions and zucchini and eaten as a side dish with meatloaf. Once again, the corn was not right. This would be Dad's final attempt. With so many farmers in the congregation, there was no need. They had the right fertilizers. He did not. The strawberries had been reaped months before and turned into freezer jam. Kevin and Tiffany had almost devoured every pint already. They had not consumed the tomatoes, but Mom and Dad had. Freshly sliced on sandwiches, they savored the bites. They had canned quarts of tomato juice. Now Dad was cleaning up and thinking about the sermon he would deliver the next day.

As he turned the tiller at the end of the row, he glimpsed the rows of firewood that had been stacked against the fence line during the spring and summer. Kevin had helped him fill pickup load after pickup load. Together they had spent hours in the woods. Dad would split, and Kevin would stack. Dad estimated that about eleven loads had been hauled and placed by the fence. He wanted to get a few more before November. Every year, the wood stove in the basement and fireplace in the living room kept the heating costs down. Plus, he enjoyed the smell. And the work was good for Kevin. He was a good son, but he could be lazy. Like today, he should be out here helping. Dad looked at his watch. It was just about 7:00 AM. He would let Kevin sleep a little longer and then get him up. A few chores needed to be completed, and then the kid could have fun.

Raising children was a heavy responsibility. Dad wanted to do it right. His own childhood had been heavy. With eight siblings, money was tight, and the family relied on the garden for food. His dad worked hard, but he also drank hard. He was not an easy man. Dad appreciated his own father, but getting close to him had taken a lot of effort. His father had passed a few months before Kevin was born. His mom visited occasionally. She could be rough, too, but she had a sweet side. She was a church lady now. Dad had never imagined that when he was young. She was a faithful attendee at a Baptist church in North Carolina.

He decided to quit tilling when the plot was halfway completed. He would do the rest the following week. After he made sure Kevin was up and productive, he would study for a bit and then spend some time with the family.

Pastoring had kept him busier than he ever imagined. People were constantly in crisis: health issues, family disputes, marriage conflicts, parenting needs. Who was he? Yes, he had trained for this. He had completed a post-graduate degree, a Master of Divinity. He was also just a man from West Virginia, raised in the holler, trying to do his best. He prayed a lot. And he studied. And he did his best to make sure people knew that he cared about them. Sometimes, his wife thought he spent a little too much time taking care of others and not enough time helping with the family. Their marriage had its own stresses. Today he would try to spend a little extra time with all of them. He was mostly ready for tomorrow anyway.

Making a final pass, he lifted the blades out of the soil and guided the tiller to the shed. A few pieces of lumber served as a ramp to get the old machine into the small, gray building with white tin doors. The space was crammed with tools and random items like bicycles and a push mower. Maybe he needed to clear this out and re-organize. No, he decided, not today. He stacked the useful pieces of wood inside the door and closed the building. He had added a padlock after a recent attempted break-in at the church. This small community was mostly peaceful, but you still had to err on the side of caution.

He surveyed the firewood again. A lot of the wood had dried out nicely. And he liked the way it was stacked. Kevin had done well, with Dad's guidance, of course. Kevin was paying attention to detail like his father. Across the fence, he noticed movement. A few deer were working their way down the hill heading for a salt block placed by the neighbor. Dad thought about hunting this fall, probably over at Art's. He missed the squirrel hunts of his youth. He needed to check his shotguns. It was probably time to teach Kevin how to shoot, too. One final deep inhalation of the cool, morning air, and he turned to the house.

Kevin was still in bed, but he was not asleep. He was reading. Dad knocked on the door and poked his head in the room.

"What are you reading?"

"A book." That kind of smart aleck answer would have angered his mother. Dad was more patient.

He gave Kevin a look. "Would you like to give me a more respectful answer?"

"Sorry, Dad. This is The Lion, The Witch and the Wardrobe. Have you read it?"

"I have not. I didn't read when I was a kid like you do. I enjoy books more now, but the only C. S. Lewis book I've read a bit is The Screwtape Letters. Have you read that one?"

"That doesn't even sound like a real thing. Screwtape?"

"Someday you might appreciate it. Right now, it's time to get some breakfast. How about pancakes?"

Kevin's face lit up. "I would get out of bed for pancakes."

"Well, then. Get dressed, make your bed and get upstairs. I may need some help." He turned to leave and then added, "Kevin, I noticed how great the firewood looked stacked against the fence. You stacked a lot of that, and you did a good job. I'm proud of you."

Kevin did not know how to respond. He always dreaded going out in the woods to collect firewood. He would rather be playing football or reading. However, he discovered that he found a lot of satisfaction in fulfilling the task. When those long hours came to an end, and he could see the enormous amount of work he had accomplished, with Dad of course, he was very proud. And then Dad just set it all on fire, several pieces at a time. By spring, the entire pile would be gone, and they would have to begin again.

"We're going to start burning it soon, aren't we, Dad?"

"Probably. We'll make sure the stove is cleaned out and ready to go but not today. Let's eat some pancakes."

Dad left. Kevin stretched and got out of bed. He pulled his white sheet up and spread the dark green comforter neatly making sure the Navajo design was symmetrical. He placed the pillows against the cool, concrete wall. He had no headboard. Finding some clean play clothes, he changed. Wearing jeans instead of the pants he had to wear to school felt great. Throwing on a fresh red t-shirt, he stopped by the bathroom before heading upstairs barefoot.

Dad had the batter started, and the griddle was warming.

"How many pancakes do you think you can eat?"

"How many are you making?"

"How about we begin with two?"

"That's a good start."

Kevin pulled out a chair from the table and sat down. Dad had already set plates and utensils on the table with butter and syrup. There were no cups. Kevin got back up and plodded over to the cabinet. He grabbed an orange plastic cup he liked. He crossed the short space of the kitchen to where his dad stood whisking the batter. He grabbed the milk from off the counter. Carefully, he opened the cap and spilled the rich white liquid into his cup. He put the cap back on and set the milk near his dad in case he needed a little more. Then Kevin got his cup and took a drink. Milk was delicious. But chocolate syrup would have made it even better. A quick search of the fridge yielded disappointing results – no chocolate milk today. He went back to the old table and took his seat once more.

The dark veneer was showing its years of wear. When company came over, leaves could be added, and the table would fill the small dining room space. Kevin's chair at family dinners was the seat against the wall with the kitchen in front of him, the window to his left and the living room to his right. He could see everything. What he saw at the moment was his sister, Tiffany, coming down the hallway. She was still in a long pink nightgown.

"Pancakes for breakfast!" Kevin exclaimed.

She smiled. "I better get one before you eat them all."

"I think I've got plenty," said Dad. "Good morning, Sis."

"Good morning, Daddy." She walked over and gave him a little hug. She stretched out on the tip of her toes and gave him a kiss on the cheek. Then she walked over to give Kevin a peck on the cheek before sitting to his right. She was in a good mood, not that she was ever in a foul mood, but still.

"Pancakes will be ready soon," Dad informed them. "Then everyone needs to get busy cleaning."

Kevin was not surprised. This was pretty much the Saturday morning routine. White glove cleaning would commence shortly. Every surface would be dusted. All floors would be vacuumed. Any clutter would be put away. Kevin was generally responsible not just for his room but for the entire basement. Sometimes he had to clean up other people's messes, like dirt tracked in from the garage. He had learned to keep his own footprint to a minimum. And he often cleaned without being asked, so that the work wouldn't take so long when required.

Tiffany had a lot of shelves in her room. Filled with books and knick-knacks, she could take hours to carefully remove them, wipe down the surfaces and return the books to their nooks. The old guy who built the house had installed a stereo with speakers in every room that could be controlled from a switchboard in her room. Mom and Dad hooked up their own stereo with tape deck, record player and radio. Sometimes, at night, Mom would have a record play a story for the children as they went to sleep. Custom became that on Saturday morning around 9:00 AM, Tiffany would set the radio to public radio that played the Boston Pops Orchestra. She would flip the switches so that the sound was playing throughout the house while everyone cleaned.

The Stephens had moved into the house when Kevin was just four years old. He remembered little of the first house the family rented in Glenford. Horrific flooding had been imprinted on his brain. He had a vague memory of standing on the second floor and seeing water on the first. There were also some memories of sharing a room with his sister and of eerie music coming from his parents' bedroom on Sunday nights after church. Turned out, they were fans of the Perry Mason show.

Kevin never thought of the internal sound system as unusual. This was normal for him. But when friends came to visit, they were shocked. This led to occasional pranks. You could turn the volume way up, turn the sound off in every room but one and blast the target with loud noise. Sometimes, his parents used it to wake him up in the morning. More often, they just yelled through the vents.

"Are you up?!" They would yell. Kevin knew that there were two meanings to this question – "Are you awake," and "Are you out of bed?" He took advantage of this flexible meaning to avoid lying. Mom and Dad were wanting to know if he was out of bed. He was stating that he was awake. Sometimes they realized they were not being specific enough and would yell, "Are you out of bed?" Kevin did not like that one. You could get in big trouble for lying. He would usually jump out of bed and holler back, "Of course!" Language is a beautiful gift, Kevin was learning.

He looked at the clock on the stove. 9:00 was fast approaching. He looked at Tiffany.

"Almost time to turn on the music."

"Yes, at least in my room. Should I flip the switch for yours?"

He glared at her. Both of them were teasing. "If you don't, I'll spray you with the sink hose."

"It doesn't reach to my room."

"I know that. I'll get you when you're in the kitchen. I'm not stupid."

"Well..." she let the innuendo hang.

"Okay, kids, first batch is ready." Dad placed a plate stacked with hot cakes on the table. Kevin reached out. "Ladies first," Dad reminded him.

Kevin took a pancake and placed it on Tiffany's plate, and then he grabbed one for himself.

"Let's pray before we eat." Dad never let a meal start without prayer. "Kevin, why don't you pray."

Kevin liked saying the prayer. He could keep it short and sweet. And he did. The final amen was like breaking the huddle in football. As soon as the word was uttered, chaos commenced. He had noticed that at church, too, especially during the final prayer. People prepared for the amen like runners readying for a starter's pistol.

Tiffany reached for the butter, but he went for the syrup. Butter wasn't necessary. Thick streams of maple syrup covered the pancake. He passed the bottle to Tiffany and got busy eating. The first was gone lickety-split, then another and another. Dad's pancakes were the best. Thick and fluffy, they soaked in the syrup. Kevin finished off his milk and sat back with a contented sigh.

Tiffany smirked. "Done so soon? Where'd you put all that?" She reached over and patted his stomach.

"Ugh, don't touch me. I'm going to explode."

"That's what I'm hoping, but please do that downstairs. I don't want to have to clean up the mess."

Dad added, "Outside would be even better." Kevin watched as his father prepared a tray of food to carry back to his mom. Breakfast would be in bed for her. Agnes, his baby sister, must be with Mom, too. He slid off the chair and laid out on the worn red carpet. Tiffany cleared the table. Dad would probably clean up the kitchen while they got started on their bedrooms.

"Can you make it down the stairs, or do I need to roll you?"

She stood over him. Normally, he would attempt a clever come-back. This morning, he could only manage a grunt.

"Well, I'm going to finish cleaning before you do," and she walked back toward her bedroom.

Kevin was competitive. Her confidence inspired him to stand up and totter down the stairs. As he moved, he felt the weight of breakfast subtly shift. By the time he stepped off the last stair, his energy was returning. He was going to be done before Tiffany. He trotted across the concrete floor, the soles of his feet feeling the coolness beneath him. He paused to grab a rag from a crock by the washing machine along with a can of Pledge. His room would be cleaner than a surgery center. By the time he got situated in his room and began to clear his shelves, the music was playing over the speakers. The theme for today was marches. One of his favorites was the Washington Post March because that was also the music on the football game he played at Sam's house. He had his own cassette player and a tape of Philip Sousa marches. The Ohio State marching band played those songs too. Plus, the peppy beat put him in a good mood. He cleaned with gusto. Before long, the shelves were dusted and rearranged. He grouped his sets of books together – the Hardy boys, Tom Swift and Sugar Creek Gang. The Chronicles of Narnia were in a paperback box collection and received special placement on the top shelf. He had his Bible and various individual books organized by size from biggest to smallest. He loved books about dogs, too. Big Red was sitting there, and a copy of Call of the Wild that Mrs. Kathy had given him. That project finished, he dusted his little memento shelf. To get to that, he climbed atop his desk. Removing the dog figurines one at a time, he carefully wiped off each individual ledge. He reset the collection and climbed down off the desk when he was finished. The desk itself was its own project. He lifted the lid and stared at the mess. Too many papers had been shoved inside in a hurry. This was a disaster. He had forgotten about competing with his sister. Now his mind was consumed with the task of cleaning and organizing his desk. He pulled out all the coloring papers and books and construction paper and crayons and pens and colored pencils. Everything was thrown on the floor. He was organizing the various sheets of paper into a pile when he heard footsteps. Because of the music, he heard them just as they reached his door. He looked up, and Mom was there.

"How's it coming?" she asked.

His heart raced a bit. "I was almost done, but my desk was pretty messy. I thought I would get it straightened up. Then all I have to do is vacuum, and my bedroom will be clean."

Mom looked around. He searched her face hoping for approval.

"Your shelves look good."

He was relieved.

"What about your bathroom?"

He groaned. "I haven't done that yet."

"And you need to sweep out here, too."

"Yes, ma'am." There was no better response to anything Mom said than, "Yes, ma'am." Anything else, and you were risking trouble.

"Did you memorize your verse for Sunday School tomorrow?"

Kevin thought for a moment. He had not worked on it since early in the week, but he thought he could still remember. "Um. Philippians 4:4. Rejoice in the Lord always: and again, I say, Rejoice." He was kind of surprised he could recall that.

Mom seemed impressed. "Good job. Do you have any homework you need to finish before Monday?"

"No, ma'am."

"Well, I'll be back to check on this desk later."

"Yes, ma'am."

"I love you," she said and walked over to the washing machine. She was going to be in the vicinity for a bit.

Kevin went back to work on his desk project. He finished the pile of papers and put those back in the desk on the bottom. He piled the coloring books, word-find puzzle and a pad of construction paper on top. Then he added back in the various pencils and markers. He like colored pencils the best. They did not bleed through thin paper like markers. Closing the desk, he looked around. Everything seemed in order. Sometimes his closet could get messy, but he knew that was currently okay. Time for vacuuming. He stepped out of his room. While he was concentrating on his organization, Mom had finished loading the washer and returned upstairs. He needed the vacuum. Just as he entertained the thought, he heard the whir of the same instrument above him. Tiffany already had her hands on it.

"Shoot." One task remained that did not require the sweeper. His gaze turned towards the bathroom. More rags would be needed and cleaning spray. Taking what he needed from the shelf near the laundry, he entered the tiny room with a toilet and sink sitting opposite each other. A medicine cabinet with a mirror hung above the sink. That mirror was splattered with toothpaste. The sink was dirty. Someone, probably two someones, had washed their hands after being out in the garden. The result was some dirt around the drain and some dried mud on the backsplash. The toilet was not horrible, but Kevin had missed the bowl while peeing in the middle of the night. He grimaced. He had to find a way to never miss. Sometimes the pee just came out in a weird way, not even in the direction he was aiming. A small rug lay on the floor between the two utilities. He pulled that aside and looked at the linoleum that was underneath. All of this needed scrubbed. So, he got busy. The mirror was first. Then he cleaned the sink. He turned to the toilet. Lid, cover, seat and base – he wiped them all down. Then he cleaned the floor around the toilet and made sure the bit of floor covered by the rug was also clean. He emptied the trash can and put the rug back in the middle after shaking it out in the utility sink. He was impressed. This looked as good as new.

He headed upstairs to get the vacuum. His timing was impeccable. Sis was finished. "I beat you, didn't I?" she gloated.

"Only because I am doing more work than you. Did you have to clean a bathroom?"

"Not yet. But yeah, Mom will probably have me do that next."

"It never ends," Kevin whispered in a low voice.

Tiffany laughed. "That's not true, Kevin. Dad was talking about playing games later. We won't be cleaning all day."

"Really? We're going to play some games?" Kevin enjoyed game nights. Sometimes Dad would make caramel corn, and they would play card games like UNO. Occasionally, they would play hide and go seek, with Mom and Dad always finding the best spots to hide. Since the baby came along, some of those routines had gone on hiatus, but as Agnes became a toddler, Mom was slowly getting back to her old self.

"Not until tonight. But maybe," she said.

Tiffany always knew a lot more than he did. That was part of the concession of being the basement-dweller. She talked to Mom and Dad more because she was right there. And she was older. She was also in Mom's crosshairs a lot more frequently. The dungeon had its benefits.

He lugged the vacuum to the stairs and made it to the landing. Somewhere in his trip up and conversation with Sis, Mom had made her way down and was now returning with a basket of laundry.

"Why don't you sweep these stairs on your way down?"

Inwardly, Kevin was pissed. Another chore? Outwardly, he knew to keep his composure. Mom could read facial expressions like Joe Montana could read defenses.

"Yes, ma'am."

He was afraid his voice had betrayed him. Mom stared at him. "Rejoice in the Lord always. That's the verse for tomorrow. Be thankful you have a house to clean and a sweeper to use."

He attempted to sound a little happier. "Yes, ma'am." Even he knew that he did not sound like he was rejoicing.

She passed him and continued to her room. Over her shoulder, she added, "I'm doing chores, too, Kevin. I'm folding your laundry."

"Thanks, Mom." He was sincere. He was truly surprised that was not on his to-do list also.

He found the outlet around the corner at the top of the stairs. He had performed this routine many times. Because the cord was not long enough, only half of the stairs could be swept before the electrical cord had to be switched to the basement outlet. He flipped the switch and rubbed the nozzle through the red carpet of the top two stairs. Then he hit the white linoleum of the landing with its welcome mat. He started down the stairs to the basement. The carpet was different on this section. Dark green was the predominant hue with patterns of embedded black. His mom hated the various carpets that the original builder had chosen. Black and white shag was used in the upstairs bathroom. In the kitchen, the old man had chosen thin carpeting with a square-within-square pattern of navy blue, red and orange. It was busy. Someday, his mother assured them, all of the carpet would be replaced. Kevin did not necessarily care. He just wished that none of it required vacuuming. He was halfway down when he tugged a bit too hard and the cord came loose. He moved the unit to the lower landing and the cord to the basement plug. Resuming his task, he methodically worked his way down the stairs to the lower landing covered in the same green carpet. Then, he completed the final two steps to the basement. The stairs were complete. He used the attachment with a long, stiff aluminum pole and broad padded head designed for hard surfaces and began to vacuum the dirt and dust from the concrete floor. The little Filter Queen unit rolled behind him. Before long the hallway floor was clean, and then the laundry area and the playroom. His bedroom was left for last. The attachment was switched for carpeting. He worked steadily with purpose, completing a task he had performed many times. At last, he finished. He switched the vacuum off and found the speaker was silent. Tiffany had turned off the music. Putting the vacuum away, he decided not to volunteer the information that he was now available for additional chores.

Instead, he slipped on some socks and shoes, went to the garage and grabbed his football. When he stepped outside, he was still in shadow, but as he ran up the hill and around the deck, the sun hit him with full force. For September, the day had become warm. He set up at the 20-yard line which was aligned with the bird feeder.

"Hike!" Karsatos dropped back and dropped a short pass to Vince Workman out of the backfield. Workman made a move over the middle, cut back to the left and leaped over a defender. The first play of the game would be a touchdown! Vince saw one last defender at the goal line and dove for the corner of the endzone. Score!

He rolled over and over down a short slope to the neighbor's wire fence. The grass felt cool and lush. When he stood, he noticed that Dad was walking through the field about a hundred yards away. He wondered what Dad was doing. He had nothing in his hands. He was just walking.

Kevin reset the game in his head.

Karsatos was under center. "Hike!" he yelled. He turned and handed the ball to Keith Byars. The run was short. Byars was tackled after a five-yard gain. Back under center, Karsatos again barked, "Hike!" He handed off to Byars again. Another short gain, and now the down was 3rd and 1. Karsatos set the play in the huddle, then turned and got under center. "Hike!" The savvy quarterback faked the handoff to the fullback and tossed it out to the flat to Byars. Keith made a man miss and was quickly over midfield to the 30, the 20, the 10. Touchdown, Ohio State!

Dad had walked all the way up the field to the backyard by now. "How about I throw you a pass or two?"

Kevin was thrilled. As much as he loved throwing the ball to himself, having Dad as a quarterback was so much better. He threw his own nice spiral to Dad who caught the ball easily. Dad had never played organized sports. When he wasn't in school, he was working on the family farm or helping neighbors. Still, he had a knack for athletics. Kevin had seen him shoot basketball and play softball. Dad could compete. Kevin took off running, and Dad set his feet and delivered a toss over Kevin's head. He jumped and got his hands on the ball midair. Falling to the ground, he rolled over and jumped up, the football tucked under his arm.

"Nice catch!"

"Thanks! I like catching tough passes." Kevin threw the ball back to Dad adding as much zip as he could. Dad was unfazed. He reached to his left and tipped the ball with one hand back to himself. Then he immediately launched another throw high but shallow. Kevin ran up under it and waited for it to fall from the sky. He made the motion for a fair catch and caught the ball where he stood. The game of pass continued for much longer than just a pass or two. Father and son alternately gave each other easy and difficult passes to catch. The ball hit the ground a few times, but for the most part, the two were catching whatever the other threw.

At last, Dad was sweaty and tired. The early hours of work were catching up with him.

"Okay, buddy, let's take a break. I think it's lunch time."

Kevin could have kept playing. He had done so many times. Football was better than food, at least for a few hours. Reluctantly, he tossed the ball under the tree and followed Dad inside.

Family lunches were rare. Supper was the meal they usually consumed together. Only on Sundays did the family normally sit down to eat a noon meal. Through the week, most days were every man for himself, or woman for herself. Today was different. Dad washed his hands at the sink and grabbed some chipped ham from the refrigerator. Kevin knew what he was doing, so he reached into the cabinet for buns. He pulled down a bag of chips, too. Tiffany entered the mix and set the table. Before long, Mom was there, too. Agnes was in her crib for a nap. The remaining four got glasses of tea, made their sandwiches and sat at the table with the chips in the middle.

Dad prayed.

Small talk ensued. Mom and Dad were concerned for Sunday. Was everything ready? Were the bulletins prepared? Was anyone singing a special? What hymns were chosen? Were any Sunday school teachers going to be absent? How many people were expected to attend? Kevin listened halfheartedly while enjoying the salty ham on the bun. The tang of Miracle Whip and the sharp dill pickles were perfect complements. He would probably have another one.

He was accustomed to the constant haranguing about church. Church was the reason their family was here in Glenford, Ohio. Church paid Dad's salary. Church was family. Church was life. Mom and Dad fussed over attendance every Sunday. Did the ushers get the count right? Was attendance better or worse than the previous

Sunday? Who was missing? Who was new? Would the new people come back?

Kevin enjoyed church for the most part. Sometimes, Dad's sermons were a bit too long. Kevin would daydream. He had learned, though, that he always needed to appear to be paying attention. If his attention waned, Dad would snap his fingers, while preaching, to arrest his attention. Or Mom would touch his knee and point forward. The best distraction was reading the Bible. You never got in trouble for reading the Bible. If Dad's sermon got boring, Kevin would flip to the Gospels and read the stories about Jesus. Or he would turn back to the Old Testament and read the stories about King David. The fight versus Goliath was epic. Kevin had heard them all. Since he was born, he had been in every church service on every Sunday and every Wednesday night. Additionally, they had extra services a few times a year called "revivals." A special speaker would be invited to preach every night for a week. Kevin had to wear a shirt and tie to each service. The adults would compliment him for looking like a young pastor. At the age of eight, he was noticing that he knew as much about the Bible as many adults.

But today was Saturday. They should save the church obsession for tomorrow. Kevin went back to the kitchen and prepared a second sandwich.

A knock at the door surprised everyone. Then the doorbell rang.

"I'll get it," said Mom. "It may be Bonnie." Bonnie was the Avon representative who lived in Glenford. Her husband was the closest thing to a celebrity that existed in the little town. Glenn played basketball for Glenford High School when they won the state championship in the late 50s.

Mom opened the door. Bonnie was not the interrupter. At the door was Sam Park.

"Oh, hi, Sam! Come on in. We're just finishing lunch. Have you eaten yet?"

"I already ate, but could I have a glass of tea?"

Mom laughed. "Yes, of course." Everyone loved Mom's tea. The Stephens used more sugar in one pot of sun tea than most people used in a month. And as people tasted truly sweet tea, they fell in love with it. "Have a seat at the table. Kevin, let Sam have your seat. Get the piano bench."

This was the way of things. Unannounced visitors were not infrequent. And they were treated well. Mom poured sweet tea into a crystal glass normally reserved for special guests. She set the tea in front of Sam. Kevin lugged the piano bench over to the dining room table. He sat on the bench more in the hallway than in the small dining room.

"Thank you," said Sam. He took a big gulp of tea. Mom grabbed the pitcher and set it on the table. He was going to drink more than one glass, for sure.

"I was headed down to church with my camera. I'm taking a photography class, and I am learning how to take some trick pictures."

"That sounds interesting," said Dad.

"I was hoping you would let Kevin go with me, so I have a subject to shoot."

"You can shoot him with a gun," volunteered Sis.

"Ha. Ha." Kevin mocked. "Only if you shoot her, too."

"Speaking of shooting," Dad interjected, "I was thinking about coming over and hunting on your property soon. Maybe I could teach Kevin how to shoot the .410."

"Oh yeah," said Sam. "Me and the Hamilton boys were target practicing a couple of weeks ago. Have you ever shot a .357?"

"I don't think I have," Dad responded.

"I'll let you give that a try. You'll be feeling that for sure."

"Hey, before I forget, I was thinking about the Christmas cantata for this year. We need to start preparing for that soon. Would you be able to help with that?"

"Absolutely," said Sam. "Let me know what you need."

He finished the glass of tea. Mom offered a refill, and he accepted.

"Do you need a key to get into the building?" Dad asked.

"I have my dad's key," said Sam. "I wasn't sure if you all were going to be around."

"Do you need Kevin to clean up for these pictures?" Mom inquired looking at his grass-stained play clothes.

"Nope. He's fine, Mrs. Stephens."

"Kevin, do you want to do that?"

Dad was letting him decide. Interesting. Dad and Mom generally decided for him.

Kevin nodded.

"We won't be there too long. I need to get this picture for a class project. I noticed there's a rocket on the wall in one of the classrooms. The picture will look like Kevin is riding the rocket."

This sounded very cool, Kevin thought.

"I'll make an extra copy for you guys," Sam offered. Then he finished his second glass. "I think I could drink a gallon of your tea every day, Mrs. Stephens."

"Well, I am glad you enjoy it, young man."

Sam stood up. He looked at Kevin. "Do you need anything, or are you ready to roll, Keverino?"

"I'm ready to roll."

"Let's go."

Sam shook Dad's hand and thanked Mrs. Stephens again. He teased Tiffany and walked down the steps and out the door. Kevin followed.

They stepped out on the deck, and the white storm door shut behind them. The screen was open.

"Be careful pulling out of the driveway," Dad ordered.

"And bring my son back by dark," Mom joked.

It was early afternoon. The sun was still high in the sky. Sam and Kevin trotted down the wooden stairs to the driveway. The gold Trans Am sat there. Kevin had never ridden in the Trans Am. He opened the door and got in the passenger seat. Sam was already behind the wheel. He fired up the engine. Neither of them put on a seatbelt. The ride down to the church was short. Sam backed into the turnaround space and then pulled forward. He eased out of the driveway so as not to kick up gravel. When he got to the road and saw no one coming, he quickly accelerated. Kevin felt the thrill of speed as Sam whisked down the highway. He wasn't going that fast, but the hum of the engine and the breeze through the open windows made 60 miles per hour feel like 90.

"You ready to drive yet?"

"Yes," Kevin replied. "It's not that hard."

Sam laughed. "Well, it doesn't look hard, but you have to be able to reach the pedals."

"I'm almost there."

"Yes. You are. You'll be driving the tractor down to mow soon, won't you?"

"I hope so."

They were already at the church parking lot and turning in. Sam parked beside the sidewalk adjacent to the building. Maranatha Bible Church met in a large, 2-story brick building. Completed just a few years before, the building had attracted a lot of attention in the community. A couple of churches already existed before Dad moved his family into town. The main church was the Lutheran assembly that met in a building on a hill just outside of the village. That auditorium had a large and beautiful stained-glass window that overlooked the valley.

Another church sat down in the town on Pearl Street. Clad with white boards, the old Brethren building had been built in the early 1900s. Maranatha rented the old structure for a while before building a new edifice about two miles down the highway on the east side of town. State Route 204 took a large turn as the road stretched east to west. Hopewell Indian Road dead-ended at the curve. The building with the large cross on the front was difficult to miss. The community was familiar with Maranatha.

The country church had begun with a Bible study in a house near town. A small group of Christians were meeting on a regular basis, but they did not have trained clergy to lead. Pastor Stephens had been introduced to the group through a preacher in nearby Newark, Ohio. Originally, Dad thought he would be an assistant to that pastor. When he moved to Glenford, he realized that the expectation was that he would transform this Bible study group into a church. From a house setting, the group moved to the Glenford high school and then to the new elementary school. Not long after, they discovered that the old Brethren building was available. And now the church had its own property and felt more official.

Kevin remembered the Brethren church well. Upstairs were the hard wooden pews, the wood-paneled ceiling and the pulpit. Downstairs was enough space for nursery and Sunday school. The old building did not have running water. The creek, or crick, as Kevin called the stream behind the church, was the source of flushing the indoor outhouses. Church members took turns emptying the plastic, five-gallon chamber pots. But people were simple and did not mind the inconvenience. More people came, and Pastor Stephens led the church in engaging with the community with activities for teens and events for families. When the time came to expand, the burgeoning congregation decided to build new. Land was donated by the Frizzell family. Dad and the church leaders put a blueprint together, and development began. Kevin did not know the details, but he did remember being on site often. He watched as the vacant plot yielded to a deep foundation. The framing went up, and the building began to take shape. Plumbing would be a welcome addition to this phase of congregational life. No one would miss the five-gallon buckets. No one. The roof went on. Electricity was installed. Brick walls slowly encapsulated the building. Drywall was hung on the interior. After months of hard work, the building was finally ready for occupancy. While the old Brethren church could seat about ninety people, the new building had room for two hundred. A large empty room downstairs adjoined a kitchen for potlucks and indoor activities. And there were classrooms for the Sunday school groups.

The church opened with a dedication service, and the entire community was invited. What they found when they parked in the gravel lot was a large stairway to the main entrance near the front of the building. A ramp to the left zig-zagged up the incline allowing handicapped access. When you reached the main door, you entered a small lobby with coat racks to the right. The walls on the left were for the pastor's study and the church office. The floors were covered in a thin, country blue carpet. As you made your way forward, you could see the nursery straight ahead with bathrooms to the left. On your right was a tiny closet for the sound booth. And then you were at the main doors to the auditorium. The dark, heavy doors swung slowly open to a main aisle with ten rows of pews on each side. Powder blue cloth with padding made these pews much more comfortable than the old Brethren hardwoods. At the front was a platform with a grand piano on the left of the audience and an organ on the right. In the middle was the pulpit. The platform was about 30 inches high. Simple windows were on both side walls providing some natural light for the parishioners. In the back of the room, behind the pulpit was an open space for the baptistry. When you got up close, you could see the giant blue tub that was only filled when Pastor Stephens was hosting a baptismal service.

Kevin knew the building like few others. He had even explored the attic through the closet entrance in Dad's study. At times, he went to church while Dad was studying. He would occasionally sit in the office and color at the desk. He knew how to answer the phone: "Maranatha Bible Church, Kevin speaking. How may I help you?"

When Sam said there was a rocket on the wall in one of the classrooms, Kevin knew exactly which one. A Sunday school teacher was using some theme that was clearly not in the Bible for some lesson or another. She had designed a simple rocket outline and placed it on the back wall. Sam grabbed his camera from the tiny back seat. Then he and Kevin jogged up twenty-two steps to the front porch. Sam fished a key from his pocket and unlocked the door. Kevin followed him inside. Sam shut the door and locked it again. They headed down the hall and to the left past the bathrooms now on the right as they opened the thick door that led to the indoor stairwell. They jogged down the steps and opened the basement door. Turning left they covered the twenty feet to the wall and turned right. Down the left-hand side were the classrooms. The wall on the right hid the janitor's closet and the first door on the right opened to the kitchen. Past the kitchen the right-hand side opened up all the way to the wall while the classrooms continued on the left. The large open area was a space Kevin enjoyed for racing his remote-controlled vehicle. "Aw," he thought, "I should've brought my car."

At the end of the open area was an exit door to the outside. The back wall could be opened up, but the space was typically a classroom. Sam and Kevin were headed to the last room on the left. Sam arrived first and flipped the light switch on. There was no exterior window in this room. The red rocket was taped to the wall. About five feet long, it was simple but clearly a rocket. Fins splayed from the back end, and the nose was a triangle. Sam set up his camera. He took a few pictures while Kevin drew on the whiteboard. In his mind, he was delivering a Sunday school lesson on Gideon and the death of King Eglon.

"Okay, boy," Sam huffed. "I am ready for you." For years, the photo that resulted floated around the family albums. Kevin, at eight years of age, standing perpendicular to the wall, his legs separated, his torso slightly hunched forward, and his arms reaching out like they are grasping the rocket as it blasts off. His head is tilted to the side, and he's smiling at the camera. He's enjoying the moment. He's just a boy.

Sam snapped a few more shots. Then he was done.

"That's it. I'll get them developed. Your picture will overlap the rocket picture, and it will look like you are sitting on the rocket."

"Cool," said Kevin.

Sam turned the light off. They retraced their steps. As they passed through the upstairs door, the men's bathroom was immediately on the left. Sam opened the door and turned the light on.

"Come on in." He stepped in and Kevin followed. He shut the door and locked it. "Remember what we did at my house?" Kevin nodded. "Take your clothes off."

Kevin shyly removed his shoes, his pants, his underwear, his shirt, and even his socks. Sam got naked, too. They repeated some of the deeds from the night in Sam's bedroom. Sam took more time pleasuring himself with his socks. There was no catalog of women to ogle.

Sam used Kevin for his pleasure. He got on top of Kevin from behind again and pushed as much as Kevin could bear.

Kevin would remember that bathroom for years to come. The walls were yellow like his room at home. The floor was a cheap tile with a mustard-based, swirly pattern of thin red and blue lines that was difficult to describe. But Kevin could see it in his mind's eye for the rest of his life. The stall to the left with the handicap rail and toilet, the sink and mirror in the middle and the urinal to the right were all permanently etched into his brain. With those images were the embedded memories of Sam's warm breath on his body and his skin against Kevin's skin. After a long session of pleasure, Sam finished in Kevin's mouth.

"That feels good, doesn't it?"

Kevin nodded.

"Maybe we can do it again sometime. But this is our secret, okay?"

Kevin nodded again.

Sam tousled Kevin's hair. "You're a good kid." And he dressed again. Kevin dressed, too. They exited the building with Sam locking the door behind him. Back in the Trans Am, Sam peeled out of the parking lot, on to the highway, and within a couple of minutes, they were back in the Stephens' driveway.

"Thanks for your help today! I think you're going to like that picture. I'll see you tomorrow."

Kevin opened the door and climbed out. "See you tomorrow."

Afternoon was fading, but the weather was still perfect. Kevin entered through the garage and went to his bathroom. He shut the door and peed. He did not miss the bowl this time. Cleaning the bathroom seemed like something that had happened long ago. Turning to the sink, he saw his reflection in the mirror, then looked down. He washed his hands staring at the sink. His brown plaid towel hung on the towel bar. He dried his hands and wandered to his room. He couldn't decide what he wanted to do, but he didn't feel like being around his family. He picked up The Lion, The Witch, and The Wardrobe, read a few paragraphs and comprehended none of it. He put it down. He changed clothes and put the ones he had worn to the church in the laundry pile. Supper time was coming soon. He had no appetite. Almost absent-mindedly, he sat at his desk and pulled out a coloring book and some colored pencils. Coloring required no focus.

Footsteps sounded in the hallway.

"Kevin, are you home?" Dad called out.

Kevin said, "Yes, sir," just as Dad got to his door.

"I figured you would come tell us you were back. Did you have a good time?"

"Yes, sir."

"Did Sam get the picture he wanted?"

"Yes, sir."

"Want to throw a few more passes before supper?"

"Sure."

"I'll put on my shoes and meet you out there."

"Yes, sir."

Kevin left the unfinished page on the desk and ambled down the hall, out the door, through the garage, outside and up the hill around the house to the backyard.

Walking over to his climbing tree, he picked up the football and tossed it in the air. When Dad popped out the door onto the deck, Kevin could hear the storm door slam. He knew Dad was on his way. He made his way out from under the tree so that his pass to his father would not be obstructed. He heaved the ball high into the air in the direction of Dad who had no problem making the catch. The toss back to Kevin was a tight spiral. He caught the football and automatically spun the oval so that his fingers were on the laces. Everything was on autopilot. He was devoid of emotion, empty of thought. Normally, this would be an exhilarating activity. This afternoon he felt nothing. Dad didn't seem to notice. Back and forth the ball flew. And then the kitchen window raised. Tiffany was inside.

"Hey, Kevin, come here. I need to ask you something."

He walked right into her trap. He wasn't even thinking about what happened a few weeks ago. She let him come all the way to the window.

"What?" he asked. He was looking up. She was elevated due to the difference between the interior floor and the exterior ground level.

"Are you ready for supper?"

"I guess."

"Would you rather have a shower?" And she sprayed him.

He could hear Mom cackling in the background. She knew what was going to happen the entire time. He ducked under the window and ran to the side. He turned back to Dad who was also laughing.

Kevin wasn't angry. He felt nothing. Well, he felt wet.

"I've gotta dry off, Dad," he said and headed back to the basement through the garage barely hearing his father reply, "Okay." He heard Dad's footsteps on the deck as he crossed through the garage. Dad was done, too.

Kevin also passed through supper listlessly. When Dad, Mom and Sis sat down to play games that evening, he participated, but he was quiet. Normally, he would tease and push the boundaries of sarcasm with Mom. But not tonight.

"Kevin, you need to take a bath before bed," Mom declared.

"Can I go now?"

"It's only 7:00, but yes, that's fine. I guess that will work well. Go ahead."

Bath time was uneventful. Undressing was awkward. He normally thought nothing of it. After all, he was alone. He also stared at his own penis while in the bathtub and touched himself. He did not play in the tub like he normally did. There was no plugging the bathtub and turning on the shower and pretending to be in a sinking submarine. He just soaked. And then he drained the tub, dried himself off, put on his plaid homemade pajamas and carried his clothes downstairs. He crawled into bed and picked up another book. This time it was Spunky's Diary about a puppy.

He was so engrossed that he was surprised to hear Dad's voice. "Are you ready for bed?"

"Yes, sir."

"Let's pray, and we can turn out your light."

Dad prayed with Kevin.

"Good night, son. I love you."

"I love you, Daddy."

In the darkness, Kevin thought about the moments in the bathroom at the church. His butt was uncomfortable. Sam had been more aggressive today and pushed a little deeper. Kevin was a little confused. He had not expected Sam to hurt him. You don't hurt people you like. But he also remembered that Sam had been happy with him when they left. Maybe Sam did not know.

Kevin felt the urge to go to the bathroom, but he did not want to get up in the darkness. Rolling over, he ignored his body and closed his eyes.

Chapter Five

Day 3

K evin was ten years old. Fourth grade was behind him. And now, he was on a big adventure. He was headed to camp for the first time. His buddies from church were excited. The teenagers went to camp every summer and came back with great stories. Now, Kevin's class was old enough to go to junior camp for students in 4th-6th grades. Starting the day, however, was not fun. Kevin was awakened at 4:00 AM by his father. Bags had been packed the night before, so he simply had to make his bed and get dressed. Everyone would be gathering at the church, but they would be riding in a large van that currently sat in the Stephen's driveway. Dad helped him carry his supplies to the van and load them in the back seat.

Camp was in wild, wonderful West Virginia. Kevin went to West Virginia frequently. Lots of family still lived there. The Stephens traveled back as much as they could. Today would be the first time he went without his parents. Sis was already there. She was a counselor. Camp was a bit further away than Nanny's and Papa's house. The ride would take about five hours. He was nervous. Even though he was excited to be like one of the teenagers, he was skittish about being in a new place and staying with strangers. Five of his fellow church friends were going along, three more boys and two girls. One of the moms would drive them over and drop them off. Dad would be picking them up at the end of the week. Apparently, this camp was rustic. Kevin had to pack his own sleeping bag, pillow, towels and wash cloth. It would be like camping out, except camp provided shelter. They called them birdhouses.

Kevin had camped out a few times with his father. One of his earliest campouts was at a men's retreat when he was only six. The terminology had been a bit confusing to him. He had made a remark to his mother that she never forgot. She had picked him up from school. In the back seat he chatted away while her mind drifted.

"And I'm not sure I should have told my teacher," Kevin rambled.

That caught her attention. "What did you tell your teacher?"

"I told her that we were taking the dog with us because Dad was borrowing a pup tent."

Mom laughed and laughed.

Kevin really did not know what to expect at Wildwood Christian Camp. But Mom and Dad had given him a bag of snacks to take along and pop to drink. So, he was bound to at least enjoy the journey. Plus, his closest church buddy, Chuck, was also going.

Donna was driving. She was Chuck's mom. Technically, she was his adoptive mother. Kevin and Chuck had known each other from their earliest memories. Roughly the same age, though Chuck was a few months older, the two had been in the nursery together and every Sunday school class since. Around the age of four, they began a weekly tradition of fighting each other after church nearly every Sunday. The teens got a kick out of this entertainment, but neither Dad nor Mom found this amusing. Kevin started receiving spankings for those fights. Before he finally surrendered and quit giving in to Chuck's taunts and instigations, the two had an epic brawl that involved guests.

The Nicky Chavers drama team came to the church to present a play. That was the Sunday morning service. Afterwards, as parishioners and guest artists left the building and stood on the lawn, Chuck and Kevin got into one of their classic spats. Pretty soon fists were swinging. The crowd took sides. Two little boys in their Sunday best stood in the yard and threw punches, grappled with each other and wrestled. Finally separated, each went to his own proverbial corner where parents meted out discipline.

There was never really a winner or a loser. Punches never seemed to connect with an eye or nose. Mostly, there were hurt feelings and dirty clothes. Kevin thought Mom was mostly mad about the grass stains. For a long time, the two boys mostly got along. Sometimes, on a Sunday afternoon, they were allowed to spend the afternoon at the other's house. They played football, if at the Stephens'. Or they ran through the woods, if at the Morrison's. One such day, they were at Kevin's house and decided to perform gymnastics on the bed. They were running and jumping onto the bed and flipping. All went well until Chuck got a little too carried away and leaped far enough to hit the concrete wall. Kevin watched as Chuck nearly stuck to the wall, then slid against the rough surface. His shirt slid up as his belly slid down, and the concrete wall left scratches down his stomach. Kevin could not help but laugh, though. In his mind, the whole thing looked cartoonish. He would remember and laugh for years at the thought of Chuck sliding down the wall like Wile E. Coyote. Smack! Slide.

The last time he swung at Chuck was for a good reason. Chuck was a year ahead of him in school. All the Maranatha kids that attended Licking County Christian Academy rode together from Glenford to Heath on an old short bus. The van was an unfortunate shade of green. Other students at the Christian academy teased them for riding in the "Booger (or Boogie) Van." The mothers took turns driving. Most of the time everyone was well-behaved. Parents practiced corporal punishment in some fashion, so the children were motivated to obey the driver and treat each other well.

Kevin was in the third grade, so this was just a year before the trip to camp. Chuck was in fourth. Chuck got to the bus before Kevin and was full of piss and vinegar, for some reason. Kevin was in an unsuspecting state. His teacher let him go from the waiting line, and he crossed the parking lot. Rounding the front of the short bus, he stepped up the front stairwell to the aisle. Chuck stood in his way.

"I need a seat," said Kevin.

"Well, you can't sit down. I won't let you."

"You have to let me sit down."

"No. I don't."

"Yes. You do!"

Chuck remained belligerent. So, Kevin jabbed him in the mouth, a simple right-hand punch that split Chuck's lip. Blood spilled out. Chuck was shocked. Kevin had not thrown a punch at him in years. Chuck grabbed his mouth, sat down and started crying. For his part, Kevin also started crying. You would have thought that he lost the fight. But he knew what was coming when he got home. Dad did not disappoint him. Kevin received a spanking. However, Chuck quit bullying him, so Kevin thought he got an okay deal.

No punches would be thrown on the trip to camp. Nor would there be any arguments. Everyone was in high spirits...eventually. The first hour or so, everyone conked back out. Then, as the sun rose, the energy level increased. By the time they crossed into West Virginia, the party was in full swing. Vacation for children is an incredible thing. Breakfast was Pop Tarts and Tootsie Rolls, Fruit Roll-Ups and M&Ms. No one was eating anything other than processed sugar. Coke for breakfast? Why not. Donna was the only parent that had to suffer through the chaos that ensued. The drive was fairly calm, in actuality. Corny jokes and annoying laughter were the worst offenses. Pitstops were few. Herding even just six children in and out of a convenience store or fast-food joint was a hassle. By 11:00 AM, they were on the last winding roads in the middle of the mountains nearing camp. The last turn into the drive that led up the steep hill to Wildwood Christian Camp was so sharp, that Donna had to drive down the road and turn around. Coming back from the opposite direction, access was a bit easier. Kevin wasn't sure the van would make it up the mountainside. He thought even Donna was sweating. But at last, they topped out on the summit. Across a wide plateau cleared of trees was the main building painted forest green.

The founders of the small Christian camp were friends of Kevin's parents named Allen and Janet Marshall. Kevin had met them a couple of times. They had two sons and two daughters. The daughters were roughly Tiffany's age, and the sons were roughly Kevin's age. Amy, Jana, Aaron and Joel were their names.

Chuck's mom parked the van randomly on the field. There was not a lot of structure to anything. This was only the third or fourth year that the Marshalls had hosted camp. This was property inherited from family. Starting a camp had been Allen's dream for a long time. As they unpacked the van, Kevin noticed the tiny cabins, or birdhouses, behind the main building. There were four of them painted the same shade of deep forest green. On all sides of the field were woods and brush except behind the main building. That side was a steep drop into a valley, and the hillside was mostly uncut native growth.

Campers entered and exited the main building as they registered for camp and found out where they were staying. Chuck's mom took the lead in marching the six of them inside to await further instructions.

At the registration table sat Kevin's sister. He had never been so happy to see her.

"Hey, Sis!" He ran over and hugged her. She was not quite that happy to see him, but she wasn't mad either, just a little embarrassed.

Allen was in the room. "Another Stephens!" he exclaimed. He turned and called his son, Aaron, over.

"Remember Kevin Stephens?"

In fact, Aaron and Kevin did not remember each other. But they got acquainted quickly. Aaron served as their guide to the guys' birdhouses on the other side of the field, far from the girls' area.

Back to the van the four boys went, while the two girls waited for Tiffany. Everyone grabbed their gear, said goodbye to Mrs. Morrison, and carried their burdens across the plateau. As they neared the woods in that corner of the property, Aaron pointed to a small green hut.

"That's the outhouse." Kevin had used an outhouse a time or two, but this would be for a whole week. He died inside just a little.

Then Aaron pointed to a crude platform roughly divided into four booths. Black plastic was stapled to boards and four PVC pipes rose above the platform, one in each stall.

"Those are the showers."

Kevin could not believe it. Privacy in the showers was practically nil. He was not ready for this. Then the news got worse. They entered a clearing with four small buildings in a rough circle. They were identical to the tiny cabins back by the main auditorium. Clothes lines were strung between each. Every birdhouse contained eight bunks. Aaron showed them to their cabins. The four were bunking separately as they would not all be on the same team. This year the theme was Army versus Navy. Kevin's grandfather was a Navy veteran of World War 2. Kevin was hoping to be a member of that team. He was not in luck. Aaron took him to one of the two Army cabins. Five other boys and an adult would be staying in this tiny bunkhouse with him. He went to the back and found a bottom bunk. When he turned around, he was not nearly far enough away from anyone. He had never been homesick in his life. Maybe he had never had a reason. This was an excellent reason. Internally, he felt anxiety like he had never known. He thought he was going to puke. Some bunks had luggage on them, but currently, he was the only occupant. He organized his stuff on and under his bunk. A man stepped into the space interrupting his thoughts. He was a big man, over six feet tall and large. He stooped to enter, and when he stood up, he filled the aisle between the beds.

"Hi! I'm your counselor, Mr. Anderson. What's your name?"

"Kevin."

"Kevin what?"

"Kevin Stephens."

"Oh, you're Pastor Stephens' son! Nice to meet you. I met your sister, Tiffany."

"Yes, sir," was all Kevin could muster.

"Well, hey! Get situated and then head back to the main building. We are going to play a game before lunch. Sound good?"

"Yes, sir."

Kevin really wanted to curl up on the wooden plank that served as a bunk. Sleep would make this disappear, at least for a while. But the adult had said to head back to the main building, and Kevin could not disobey.

He decided to find Aaron again. At least he had a friend that was comfortable here. Maybe Aaron could help him get comfortable, too. Stepping down out of the birdhouse, he looked around the encampment to see if Aaron was still around. He did not see him. He saw Chuck instead. They greeted each other like long lost cousins after surviving a tornado.

"What's your cabin like?" Kevin inquired, then felt immediately stupid. How different could these four buildings be? It's not like one of them was hiding a basketball court and a hot tub.

"It's small," said Chuck.

"Yeah," agreed Kevin. "My counselor said to head over to the main building. Are you ready to go?"

"Yep."

They were joined by Jason and Jamie, the rest of their group, as they crossed the camp.

"Know what game we're playing?" Kevin asked.

No one knew.

A male counselor was standing on the deck outside the auditorium shouting instructions.

"Come on in and have a seat!"

They entered and slid into one of the 8 pews that made up the seating for the room. Auditorium was a generous word. The room could hold fifty people very uncomfortably whether adults or children. Word was that about forty kids were here for camp. Kevin was shy, but he paid close attention to the people around him and began picking up names. A few girls came in, and he was happy to see a cute girl make eye contact with him. Still, he was stressed. This was a lot. Into the room came a short, stocky man. With him, apparently his wife, was a cute woman a couple of inches shorter. She was smiling and happy. He looked serious. Stepping to the podium, he introduced himself.

"Welcome to Wildwood! I am Cary Grant. This is my wife, Paula. We are about to make a few introductions, and then we will have our first activity before lunch. Is everybody ready to have fun?!"

Kevin wasn't sure Cary was ready to have fun. And he most surely wasn't. He was about to puke.

The rest of the campers and counselors trickled in, Kevin's sister among them. Cary introduced the staff and the teams. Cheers were included. Efforts were made to get everyone up on their feet and cheering. Kevin followed along, but he was on the verge of tears. Camp was a bad idea.

Finally, they dismissed everyone outside for the first game, kickball. Kevin was relieved that the game was familiar and something at which he could excel. His first at bat was a big kick that got him to second base and scored a run. For a while, he was distracted from the knot of fears in his stomach. Lunch was good. Mrs. Marshall and her helpers had prepared mac and cheese covered with pizza sauce, pepperoni and cheese. He had never had anything like this before, and it was delicious. He was so thankful the macaroni wasn't green.

After lunch was the first devotional. This would be a lot of camp. Every day, Cary and Allen would be preaching. Kevin had already sat through thousands of sermons. Between attending church and Christian school, he had heard men speak on every subject from Jonah and the Whale to the Samaritan woman to the lawyer in 2 Timothy. Kevin did not mind a good sermon. In his opinion, the best speakers told good stories and made a few jokes. Cary's devotional was not great judged by those criteria. Plus, everyone was sleepy.

Back outside they trooped through more activities. Kevin did pretty well in the athletic competitions. All those hours of throwing the football in the backyard had honed his hand-eye coordination. The afternoon flew by. At 4:00, there was a break to get cleaned up for dinner and the evening service. Then Mr. Marshall stepped forward with a final announcement.

"After the service tonight, there will be a special activity for the guys." As he spoke, a wry grin tweaked at his lips and cheeks. He was enjoying the secrecy. Kevin stared at him without glee. Allen wore glasses, and his mostly gray hair was combed similarly to Kevin's dad's. The feathered hair on his forehead bounced up and down as he moved. Kevin could only imagine what the surprise would be.

Upon dismissal, the boys trickled across the field to their meager accommodations. Kevin reached his cabin but had to wait for a minute to enter. The little birdhouse was full. Seven people in a space barely larger than the Morrison's station wagon was a disaster. Finally, he got in. Mr. Anderson introduced him to everyone. His memory was usually sharp but not today. His belly was a bundle of nerves, and his brain short-circuited. Every fiber of his being was telling him to get out of there. But where could he go? Would Nanny and Papa come and get him? Mom and Dad would never allow that. His eyes filled with tears, and he hustled to his bunk and hid in shame. He could not let the other boys see him cry. At that moment, he both wanted his parents and hated them. Why would they send him here?

He needed a shower. Dirty and sweaty from the games, he wanted to be fresh for dinner and the service. You never went to church dirty. And what he knew of girls was that they liked guys to be clean, too. He grabbed his toiletry bag, towel, washcloth and change of clothes. By the time he reached the showers, there was a line. A breeze was blowing the plastic, and they were useless as privacy curtains. Kevin stared in the opposite direction for a bit. At last, it was his turn to take the next available stall. He prayed for something on the end. He was not that lucky. The third stall opened up. He entered and hung his towel on a nail. A rough bench allowed for his clothes. He got naked hiding behind every inch of plastic he could possibly use. He turned the water on and a tiny stream of freezing water trickled down. He might as well have taken an ice cube to his skin. Struggling to hide his nakedness while simultaneously washing himself with as little water as possible was futile. Then, as he turned to his right toward the fourth stall, a stiff breeze pulled the curtain, and he got an eyeful of Dwight, one of the adult male counselors. Dwight was comfortable with his naked body. He was bent forward with his back to the shower. He had his hands on both butt cheeks and was spreading them wide and allowing the icy water to trickle down his crack. Kevin saw everything that he never wanted to see again. In the blink of an eye, the image was tattooed on his brain. He turned away, but the damage was done. The nausea returned. He finished his pitiful shower, threw on fresh clothes and headed back to the box. He sat on his bunk, closed his eyes and covered his face with his hands. This had been a long week. And it was Monday.

Dinner was not as delicious as lunch. Salad was offered along with a five-bean chili. He ate but unenthusiastically. He said hi to Sis, but she was busy with her campers. The cute girl introduced herself as Leslie. Even that did little to boost his spirits. He had to make the trek back to the cabin to grab his Bible for the service. He sat on his bunk for several minutes, trying to make sense of this misery. Mr. Anderson entered. Seeing Kevin alone, he stepped over and put his hand on his shoulder. Kevin recoiled as he looked up. Ken had rarely experienced a reaction like that from a child. This kid did not want to be touched. He stepped back.

"Are you okay, Kevin?"

"Yes, sir."

"You looked like you were having fun during the games. You helped us win the kickball game!"

"Yes, sir."

Ken was at a loss. He wasn't getting much out of this boy.

"If you need anything, let me know. I'm glad you're in my cabin."

"Yes, sir."

At least he was polite, thought Ken.

Kevin picked up his Bible, a notebook and a pen. Trudging across the field, he entered the auditorium. Aaron was already there. Kevin sat next to him.

Aaron whispered, "I heard Leslie likes you."

Kevin blushed. "Whatever. She barely knows who I am."

"Well, she thinks you're cute."

"Doesn't matter. My parents aren't going to let me date until I'm thirty."

Aaron laughed. "Same here."

Once again, the early birds were waiting for the stragglers, but at 7:00, Mr. Marshall started the service. They sang some songs. Emotions were bubbling up inside of Kevin like Mentos in a Coke bottle. The only outlet that he could permit was crying. He was so embarrassed. Bowing his head, he hoped no one would notice. Every moment of prayer was welcome. At least then, all eyes were closed. The windows to his left showed that the sun was sinking in the western sky. Cary stepped in and preached. Kevin listened. But his eyes leaked at the corners the entire time. Kevin just wanted to get back to his bunk and go to sleep.

At last, the service concluded. Mr. Marshall stepped behind the lectern.

"I want all the guys to go change into some clothes you don't mind getting dirty. Grab your sleeping bags and meet me back here in ten minutes. Go!"

The instructions were clear but left everyone with a lot of questions. Why the guys only? Where were they taking their sleeping bags? This adventure continued to spiral.

In the birdhouse, there was the struggle of seven earthworms in a thimble. Seven guys changing in the dark in the square footage of a bathroom stall was bedlam. As each finished and grabbed their sleeping bag and headed out, the pandemonium gradually subsided. Mr. Anderson and Kevin were the last two to grab their sleeping bags and depart. They still made it back to Allen safely within the ten-minute constraint.

Mr. Marshall had a pack on his back.

"Follow me!" he yelled. And he took off hiking down the steep hill behind the auditorium. Kevin remembered that Dad had told him Mr. Marshall was a Marine in the Vietnam War. This did not bode well.

Down the steep incline and then up the other side, Kevin soon lost all sense of where camp was. They were on the mountainside far from the bunkhouse and far from Glenford, Ohio. Kevin did not know how long they traipsed through the woods nor did he have any inkling how far. If someone had told him that they had hiked 9 miles in 3 hours, he would not have been surprised. At the head of the column, Allen was talking. Kevin was toward the rear and had no idea what information was being shared. Frankly, he did not care. His small frame was filled with anger. Why had his parents sent him on this terrible expedition? He caught sight of Dwight and nearly threw up. This was hell. He was convinced God was judging him.

Eventually, Allen decided to stop. Kevin was hopeful that maybe they were back at camp. Or maybe there would be a campfire and s'mores. But no. Allen pulled them into a circle and said, "Find a place to lay your sleeping bag. We're sleeping here tonight."

Kevin had heard some sermons about the Israelites and complaining. Most of them had been uttered by his mother. She had an entire anthology of sermons on the subject in her brain. Kevin heard some complaints tonight. This was a strange introduction to Wildwood and a terrible initiation into Christian camping. Kevin needed to let his frustration out which meant finding a quiet place to cry. Finding privacy here was not difficult. He marched away from the group a stone's throw, rolled out his sleeping bag, crawled inside and let the tears out. The ground had seemed flat when he chose the spot. Now that he lay down, there were roots and rocks everywhere. He could find no way to get comfortable. More reasons to cry. He sobbed into the crook of his elbow and, at last, fell asleep.

Chapter Six

Day 4

Awaking to an alarm clock was probably the least favorite part of Kevin's day. 7:00 AM. He hit the off switch, rolled on to his back and stretched. With a yawn and a groan, he got out of bed. Nearly a teenager, Kevin was enjoying the last summer before Junior High commenced in just a few weeks. Sixth grade had been a disastrous year academically but a hilarious year socially. His teacher had been a noob, Mr. Chancey.

"Take a chance with me, and add a Y," was the goofy teacher's continual joke.

Christian schools are not known for their vigorous academic requirements for teachers. Tim Chancey was part of a package deal with his wife, Eleanor. Mrs. "Take a chance with me" was a science teacher with master's level credentials. With his auburn mustache and large glasses, Tim looked like an attendant at Jiffy Lube with assistant management aspirations. Eleanor was the home room teacher for the eighth-grade class and taught the science curriculum for Junior and Senior High. Tim was given the sixth grade. He got steamrolled. From day one, the students knew he had no will to maintain discipline. Just enough self-control reigned that the class was not in complete chaos, and occasionally some learning still took place. Usually, this required Mr. Chancey to lose his temper and threaten repercussions.

They conned him into letting them have water bottles in the room. Then they had water fights when he faced the board, and his back was toward them. They abused the restroom pass. His supplies would mysteriously disappear and reappear in unexpected places. He was cajoled into longer recesses and movies instead of class. They talked him out of quizzes and got him to grade some difficult tests on a curve. Sixth graders could be merciless. They were a pride of lions, and he was a lame gazelle.

All year long there were incidents, highlighted by Matt Holtz getting sent to the principal's office for yelling at the disliked teacher. "You son of a bish!" he screamed at a controversial call during a kickball game at recess. Matt's argument was that "bish" was not even a word. Mr. Chancey's argument was that he was tired of the disrespect. That was fair. Kevin mostly behaved himself. He did talk a lot under his breath. His humor and sarcasm had classmates laughing on a daily basis. But Kevin still feared the discipline he might receive at home, if he got in trouble at school.

Mr. Chancey did not know how to teach. Kevin passed all of his classes with honor roll recognition because he was a high-level reader. He ignored Tim at the front of the class, skimmed the textbooks and passed the tests. School was easy.

Kevin had been warned that Jr. High would be different. His sister had just one year left. Her senior year and his seventh-grade year would put them in the same building and chapel services. She was holding her breath that he would not embarrass her. She was also attempting to coach him to success.

"Miss Kinner is very strict, Kevin. I have seen her throw erasers at students for not paying attention and for asking dumb questions. You better behave around her." Susan Kinner was the seventh-grade home room teacher and taught all the math curriculum. A short lady with gray hair who looked like she had been seventy-five years old for the past twenty years, Susan was known for her outbursts in class.

Kevin was apprehensive about being near Miss Kinner every day. He was nervous about many of the changes that would take place as he entered his teen years. He was excited, too. Soon, he would be driving. He would have a job. He would be independent. But not today. Monday had arrived, and he was still a twelve-year-old kid.

He was halfway dressed before the fog cleared from his brain, and he remembered why his alarm was set. Nanny and Papa had come up for church yesterday, and he was going with them back to West Virginia. Selecting a simple blue t-shirt, he shrugged into the material and hit the bathroom before jogging upstairs. Mom and Dad had slept on the sleeper sofa in the living room, but there was no evidence. They had been up for a while. Nanny and Papa were already at the kitchen table, sipping hot coffee and waiting for Dad to fry some bacon and eggs. Mom was about to head to work. She was a registered nurse. Two or three days a week, she worked at a doctor's office in Granville. The commute was about thirty-five minutes. While the office did not open until 8:30, she liked to be early. Kevin didn't really know what Mom and Dad disagreed over. He did know that they were fully on the same page about punctuality. Thirty minutes before start seemed to be the family rule. The only exception was school. They could cut that pretty close sometimes. On Sunday mornings, the entire Stephens family would be in the church building around 9:00, even though Sunday school did not begin for another thirty minutes. The evening service began at 7:00. The Stephens arrived at 6:30. So had been the pattern for years.

Mom gave hugs to Nanny and Papa. She kissed Dad. She yelled down the hallway to Tiffany and Agnes, "I'm leaving. I love you. Be good!"

Her last hug was for Kevin. "I love you. Obey Nanny and Papa, and be a helper." She grabbed lunch off the counter and walked down the indoor stairs to the garage. A moment later the hum of the opener was audible as the door lifted on its tracks. An engine sputtered to life. Mom backed out and hit the controller in the car. The heavy door slid back into place.

Kevin stood between Nanny and Papa and wrapped an arm over each shoulder. "Good morning! When are we leaving?"

Papa laughed. "Not until I've had some bacon and eggs and another cup of coffee."

Papa seemed like the tallest person Kevin knew. He was about six foot three inches, and he had already begun to shrink slightly as he aged. Nanny had always been little. Her white hair was permed, and she wore her translucent-rimmed glasses.

"I hope you're ready to work," she said. "I have a list of things for you to do."

Kevin doubted that was true. "As long as you feed me chocolate pie, I don't mind."

Nan's chocolate pies were the best morsels of food that had ever touched Kevin's lips. Only Nan made chocolate pudding pie for him. Mom had some good desserts, too, and her Mississippi Mud Cake was a favorite. But no one made chocolate pie like Nanny. Any time he went to her house, a pie would be ready. Normally, she made one the morning of his arrival. When he walked through the main door into her open living room, dining room and kitchen, the pie would be sitting on a cooling rack on the counter. Last year, he had walked in, and the counter was vacant. Saying nothing, he turned right into the dining room and out of sheer accident saw that she had hidden the pie on the bay windowsill. He grabbed the pie and went to the kitchen to slice a piece.

Papa loved to tell that story. "Ol' Kev, he walked into the room, put his nose in the air and smelled that pie right away. She couldn't fool him one bit."

Mom's parents were West Virginians through and through. Papa and Nanny were from Elkins. They had moved to Clarksburg and built a house during Mom's childhood. Papa had served in the Navy during World War II and then worked a number of jobs including a stint in the coal mines. His large hands were rough and calloused. His speech was marked by Appalachian colloquialisms. Kevin loved his grandparents. And he often slid into the same pattern of speech when he was around them.

Dad was ready to start serving. He was close with his in-laws. They had been family to him for a long time. He made sure Nanny and Papa were taken care of and then prepared a plate for his son. Kevin slipped into a chair.

Papa grinned at him. "We better say grace."

"Grace," Kevin said. They laughed. Dad was not as amused. Dad led in a blessing.

"Amen," said Papa. "Now eat til you bust."

"Yes," Nan added, "we won't be eating again until we get home."

Kevin wasn't worried. Driving from here to Nanny and Papa's took about three-and-a-half hours. While Papa might be in a hurry to get home, he might also want to have lunch at Long John Silver's. Kevin hoped so. He did not get there often, and the hush puppies were delicious. Plus, he couldn't get enough of the battered crumbs.

Tiffany and Agnes entered the room and hugged their grandparents. Then they shared the piano bench that had been set at the far end of the expanded table. They were a juxtaposition. Tiffany was a young lady. Thin with dark medium-length hair, she was demure. Academics were important to her as was playing the piano. She played in church frequently. Her features were thin. She was pretty.

Agnes was just five years old. Her face was still full of baby fat, and she smiled and laughed with the carefree disposition of a youngest child. As the baby, she took a lot of teasing. But she also received a lot of gifts and attention.

"I want to go with Nanny and Papa, too," she was currently pouting. Dad patiently explained for the umpteenth time, that he would take her later in the week. Kevin was going early to help Papa with some chores.

Kevin didn't really care. He was just happy that he got some alone time with his grandparents.

Dad brought a stack of buttered toast to the table. Papa never ate a meal without bread. An open jar of strawberry freezer jam sat by Papa's plate.

"I heard these strawberries are fresh from the patch," he said to Kevin.

"Yep! We picked a bunch this summer."

"I was down at the garden with your dad this morning. He said you have been doing most of the weeding. I might have to have you help me get my weeds under control."

"I can do that," said Kevin. "I just need a hoe and ten dollars." He winked at Papa.

Papa chuckled. "Ten dollars! When I was a kid, we worked all day for a nickel." He paused and stared his grandson in the eyes. Then he added, "And we were grateful for that nickel."

"Bought you a bottle of pop, didn't it, Papa?" Kevin had heard these lines before.

"A soda was a quarter, but you were lucky to have a quarter." Papa and Nanny both had the best mischievous looks when they were teasing and joking.

"I didn't see a quarter until I was 9 years old," Nan said. Kevin wasn't sure if she was still joking.

"Okay, I'll do it for a bottle of soda," Kevin conceded with another wink.

"How about a can of Big K?" Papa negotiated.

"Deal. Oh, and a chocolate pie."

Nanny laughed.

As they finished breakfast, Kevin helped to clear the table. As Tiffany started to wash dishes, he ran downstairs and quickly packed. He threw his bag of clothes and books into the back seat of Papa's unlocked Oldsmobile. The dark blue Century was pretty nice, Kevin thought.

He went up the outdoor staircase to the deck and entered the house through the main door. He leaped over the two stairs and hit the red carpet. He halted immediately. Nanny and Papa were sitting on the living room sofa listening to Tiffany play one more song. Agnes snuggled on Papa's lap. She was still in her maroon-striped onesie pajamas. Tiffany was leaning into the keys as her fingers skimmed back and forth. This was a piece by Rachmaninoff that she had performed for state competition in April. She needed no sheet music. Her muscle memory was still perfect from her second-place finish. Next year, she was determined to place first. The guy who beat her had graduated.

With a flourish, she concluded the composition. Nanny and Papa cheered and clapped. Agnes clapped, too. Kevin was always impressed. He played the piano, too, but not nearly as well.

"Do you have something to play?" Nan asked him.

"Not really."

"Oh, come on," urged Papa. "We know you are working on some-thing."

"Not like Sis."

"Well, that doesn't matter. Just play us whatever you're learning."

"I could play something for you on my trumpet," Kevin volun-teered.

"That works for me," said Papa.

"Do I need to cover my ears?" asked Nan.

"Yes," confirmed Agnes.

Tiffany laughed. "He's better than he used to be. I used to think a cow was dying in the basement."

Kevin had started trumpet lessons in the third grade after his teacher, Bethany, had introduced the class to one of her friends. Dave Birros was a graduate of The Ohio State University. He played trumpet and had even been a member of The Best Damn Band In The Land. His performance for Kevin's class had been riveting. He played a few songs including the classic march, Across the Field. Then he drank a raw egg out of a glass. Bethany had made many impressions on her students. She loved ice cream with the passion of a drowning man for air. Every day at lunch, she turned the radio up and had the class listen to Paul Harvey. Her grandparents came to visit. Her brothers brought in a feast of wild game around Thanksgiving. But Dave, Dave was the highlight of third grade for Kevin.

Technically, Kevin did not have a trumpet. His parents had purchased a B-flat cornet. The fingerings were the same, but Kevin had to mentally adjust the key to C when playing along with a pianist. He was beginning to do this with ease.

Most of the songs he played were hymns. He went over and opened his instrument case, pulling out the brassy cornet. He inserted the mouthpiece and blew some air through the long, complex tubing.

Rattling the three keys with his three middle fingers, he made sure they were moving smoothly.

"This is going to be loud," he announced.

"Maybe you should play from the downstairs landing," Tiffany suggested.

That was a good idea. He trotted down the stairs, warmed up with an exercise and then launched into Guide Me, O Thou Great Jehovah.

He loved music. More than tooting the notes, he was singing the song through the instrument. His pauses were meaningful, his cadences matched the words and the tone of the hymn. Having only played for a couple of years, he was playing well.

He held the final note dramatically and then inhaled deeply and walked back up to the living room.

"Yay!" yelled Nan and clapped. Papa clapped.

Kevin bowed deeply.

Even Tiffany allowed herself to compliment her little brother. "Pretty good. What was that, Amazing Grace?"

He shook his head and smiled. He knew she knew. She smirked.

"Okay, Agnes, it's your turn," Papa growled as he tickled her.

"I can play the piano." She hopped off his lap and went to the old studio instrument that had sat there since they moved in eight years ago. With confidence, Agnes tapped out Mary Had a Little Lamb.

Papa and Nanny were just as pleased with her performance as with Tiffany's classical concert.

"Well," said Papa, "We better hit the road."

The farewells were loving and sweet. Hugs and kisses were exchanged between grandparents and the two granddaughters. Dad came out of his bedroom to say goodbye. Kevin received hugs and kisses, too.

His dad parted with a final, "I love you. Be good. Be a helper."

Nanny, Papa and Kevin strolled down the stairs to the basement, walked through the garage and stepped out of the cool garage air into the warm summer morning. Kevin ran to the car and occupied the entire rear seat. He did not have to share any space with siblings. Nanny got in the passenger seat and buckled up. Papa lowered his tall frame into the driver's seat and pulled his long legs inside the door frame. He slammed the door shut, found his seatbelt and fastened the buckle. He turned the key over in the ignition and backed into the turnaround space. With a gnarled fist, he shifted the transmission into drive and headed out of the driveway.

Kevin had no sense of homesickness. The brutal week at Junior camp a couple of years ago had cured him of that. He had survived and even returned to camp every summer since. Looking out the window at the corn fields and dairy cattle, he was happy to leave home for a bit. This would be fun.

Papa and Nanny made small talk about their brief visit with Kevin occasionally chiming into the conversation. They reminisced about the church folks they had caught up with at the previous day's services. Papa knew some of the men from helping with the building. The foldable door in the basement that allowed a classroom to expand into part of the fellowship hall had been Papa's idea and execution.

From Kevin's house to the interstate was a fifteen-minute drive. Once on I-70, the miles passed in quick succession. Across the middle of Ohio they headed east until they connected with I-77. Papa took the exit south towards Marrietta. Forty-five minutes later, they crossed the Ohio River into West Virginia. Papa stopped in Parkersburg, just beyond the river.

"We're back in wild, wonderful West Virginia." He pulled into a gas station.

"I can pump the gas for you, Papa."

"Well, that'd be nice."

Kevin knew the drill. He opened the tiny door and unscrewed the gas cap. He placed it on the trunk where he would not forget to put it back. He lifted the green rubber-covered handle and inserted the heavy aluminum nozzle into the tank. Flipping the pump switch on, he selected the fuel and squeezed the handle. Gas began to flow. He watched as the cost increased. Gas was $0.89 a gallon. Papa watched with him to see what the final tally would be. Automatically, the handle clicked off - $11.64. Papa walked off to pay the attendant. Kevin removed the nozzle and hung it back on the pump flipping the switch back off. He screwed the cap back on and shut the lid. He was helping.

"Do you need anything?" asked Nan.

"I'm okay," said Kevin. Truth was, he was still full from breakfast.

Papa came back and went through the same routine of pulling himself into the car and taking off.

"Thanks for pumping the gas. That's nice," he stated. "Nan and I aren't as young as we used to be."

Kevin couldn't remember them at any other age. They seemed frozen in time, forever 80 or however old they were. He didn't even know. He probably should.

They were no longer traveling on I-77. They took Highway 50 from Parkersburg all the way to the outskirts of Clarksburg. Ninety minutes later, Papa turned left over the divided highway onto Wilson Run Road. Kevin had read a Hardy Boy mystery for much of the drive, but now he put the book away. He knew they were close. And he now knew there would be no stopping for lunch at Long John Silver's. The road wound up into the hills. Kevin recognized various houses and landmarks. He watched for the tell-tale Isaac Creek Road. On an incline, they approached the driveway. Directly across from where Isaac Creek Road tied into Wilson Run was where Papa's driveway began. By the time you took the sharp right turn into the driveway, you were past the house. As Papa made the turn and the drive straightened in front of them, Kevin could see the house up the hill on his left. The hill was neither steep nor high. A mere rise of fifteen feet or so from the driveway, you could enter the house one of two ways.

Papa had created concrete tracks up the hill just past a huge locust tree. From there you could park on a concrete pad and step into the house through the main door. This was where company generally entered. As you walked the short sidewalk to the porch, a massive rock sat beside a towering oak. The rock was a favorite place for the grandkids to play. They had seven, two boys and five girls, born into the family from their three children.

Nan's porch had a few sets of wind chimes. She enjoyed the tinkling tones when the breeze blew. If you entered at the upper level, you were stepping into the living room on the left side of the home. The space was open into the dining room to the right, and you could see into the kitchen. The rooms were small but cozy. Walls were covered in dark wood paneling. The entryway was tiled, but the floor was carpeted in beige from the living to the dining room. As you stood at the entrance, taking in the house, a door was opposite you between the main rooms. That door led to the attic which was surprisingly spacious. You could also see down the hallway that connected to the back bedrooms and the side room that served as family den and guest room. The kitchen connected to that hallway, too. And there was yet another door. The mirror-opposite of the door that led to the attic, this one led to the basement.

Papa did not park on the upper level. He continued to the garage. Similarly to Kevin's house, Papa had a full basement, and the ground sloped away about halfway down the length of the house exposing the ground floor. Papa's house was sided with pale yellow vinyl. As he pulled onto yet another concrete pad that covered about sixty square feet in front of the garage, Papa pointed to the garden further down the hill, just about thirty feet away to the right.

"I am going to need your help with that," he informed Kevin. The garden was long and somewhat narrow. Roughly the same size as the plot Kevin worked at home, the rows were tighter and fuller. Papa was not as meticulous as Dad. He did leave enough space to be able to till between the rows. Currently, the weeds were taking over.

"Yes, sir."

"But not today," Papa clarified.

They all got out of the car slowly, stretching and feeling the air. Between the house and the road were trees and a hillside covered in brush. A lot of shade was provided by the abundance of mature elm, maple, locust and oak. Papa's property included a good bit of lawn, but less than a hundred feet from the back of the house, you could enter the woods. There was a neighbor up the hill but no neighbor behind for a long distance. Back in there was a river, too. Kevin had hiked there a few times with his cousin.

Kevin grabbed his bag from the back seat, while Papa and Nanny grabbed their small suitcase and toiletry bags from the trunk. Papa had added on to this end of the house. There were now two garages. The furthest was largely filled with firewood. The original garage included a shop area in the back with Papa's tools scattered everywhere. Nanny and Papa had two different styles of organization. Nanny believed in cleanliness and organization with all her heart. Papa was an atheist. Nan ruled most of the house. Papa had his shop.

They went through another door into the basement. A small bathroom was immediately on the right. Papa could clean up there before venturing into the rest of the house.

On the left-hand wall was counter space. Papa kept beehives, and on this counter, he would drain the honeycomb and pour the golden sap into jars. There was also a sink and a spare refrigerator. On the back wall as they made their way to the staircase, Kevin could see the small door that opened to the cellar. Papa stored potatoes in that space and who knows what else. Kevin rarely stuck his head in there. On the right, past the bathroom was some open space under the stairway. A large freezer sat there, full of venison and vegetables and a tub of ice cream, at least, Kevin hoped.

They turned to go upstairs, and the rest of the tiny basement was before them. Papa had a bed down there, a chair and a wood stove. He could enjoy some rest while still dirty from being outside without having to get cleaned up first. The unfinished wooden stairs were tight, and the three of them took turns going up to the kitchen. Nanny led. She opened the door at the top of the stairs and stepped onto the linoleum flooring. Papa stepped through and headed to the bedroom.

"You can stay in the TV room," Nan told Kevin as he reached the first floor. "Crystal was in the guest room the other night, and she might be back soon. We'll keep that room for her." Crystal was one of the grandchildren, the only one that lived nearby.

Kevin didn't mind. While there was an outside door that led to the backyard, he was no longer scared of the dark. He would sleep on the small taupe-striped pull-out sofa that would fill the tiny room with a twin-size bed. With a recliner on one side and rocker on the other, space was tight even before you pulled out the cot. The wall that adjoined the living room had a closet that extended halfway. The rest of what would have been closet space, was open with a large bookcase. The antique shelves were filled with volumes large and small including a set of classic hardcovers that Kevin had read over the years. His favorite was a retelling of Robin Hood. The television stand sat in the space between the closet doors and the bookcase nook.

Near that nook, just behind the outside door when you went to step outside, sat the old leather rocker that had once caused Kevin some of the worst physical pain of his life. A few years prior, he had taken it upon himself to move the heavy chair deeper into the recess, closer to the bookshelves. With bare feet, he pushed and pulled the chair. In the process, he got his foot under the base and managed to tear the nail off his big toe. Even Nanny, the veteran of hundreds of incidents with kids and grandkids, was aghast. She helped staunch the bleeding and forced him to soak the toe for a bit in Epsom salts. She bandaged his foot and sent him to bed. He ended up on crutches for a few weeks because pressure on the toe in any manner was too painful. He side-eyed the old chair as he put his bag in the closet. That would never happen again, he swore. He slid the chair back now while he was wearing shoes. Taller and stronger, he moved the chair with ease and wondered once more how that tragedy ever occurred.

He opened the door and went out onto the covered porch with a picnic table. Then he headed left to the big rock. When he was a child, the rock was a veritable mountain. As he grew, the rock slowly shrunk. Yes, the ancient boulder could still hold all seven grandchildren and a few more easily. But climbing the side no longer felt like a feat. The end nearest the tree was roughly two feet high. At the further end, nearer the drive, the rock was about four feet high. At the base, the rock sloped down, flattened out briefly and then curved under the earth. He walked up and stood at the pinnacle facing first towards the driveway and the large field above him that sloped slowly upwards towards the crest of the hill. An old concrete block garage stood there. Not for the first time, he wondered who it belonged to and what it held. Then he turned to the right towards the woods. Another small outcropping of smaller boulders stood near and just inside the stand of trees. Kevin turned further to his right and looked down the hill. The garden was to his right past the house. To the left were the beehives Papa tended. A row of six boxes looked innocent enough from a distance. If you walked closer, as Kevin often had, you could see thousands of tiny bees flying in and out of the hives. Kevin always gave the hives a generous berth when he walked in that direction. He had experienced his share of stings at home. Oddly, he had never been stung here. Papa was fearless, of course, but he was also wearing a hat with a mesh net covering his neck and face. He always wore long sleeves and gloves, too. Holding a smoker in his hand, he would puff the smoke toward the bees. Kevin did not understand the intricacies of how the smoke affected the insects. He just knew that Papa could then open the boxes and retrieve the honeycomb. Kevin's favorite part of the process was drizzling fresh honey on his toast. Past the hives were two old sheds. Kevin had never asked Papa about the history. They were clearly much older than the house and must have been here when Papa bought the property. A rusted-out tractor sat in one. Various odds and ends could be seen in the other. Kevin never had occasion to fetch anything out of either one. The tools Papa used most often, including his hoe, were in the garage.

Being here alone was different. Usually, a cousin or two would provide companionship. At the least, Agnes and Tiffany would be joining him on the rock. They liked to play a game of tag that was called Shark. All the rocks were bases. You could only be tagged when you were not touching one of the many rocks. Whoever was "it" was the shark.

Kevin wandered down off the rock and ventured slowly down to the garden. He recognized many of the plants without effort. Papa mostly had the same stuff that Dad grew back home. Beets were something Dad never planted, Kevin thought, as he noticed that Papa had a row of them. Ugh. Beets were gross. Nan pickled and canned beets and brought them to the table as a side for most meals. Kevin did not think they tasted good at all. Most of the rows needed maintenance. Kevin wondered if Papa would let him use the tiller. That would certainly make the chore go quicker. He would ask.

He continued his walk past the garden to a patch of blackberries that Papa also tended. Papa had several fruit trees on the property, too. He liked to graft varieties of apples together. Even now, Kevin could see the white wrap on a nearby tree where Papa had spliced the branches together. What was Papa growing now?

Kevin looped back along the edge of the woods and headed back up the hill. Searching for the path to the river, he finally found what he was looking for. Weeds had overtaken the trail but the imprint was unmistakable. Maybe he would head to the river this week. He stayed out of the high grass for the moment. Ticks were not uncommon, and he did not want to be an unsuspecting host. Back to the house, he met Nan just as she was coming out to yell for him.

"How about a sandwich for lunch?" she inquired.

"That works for me."

Papa was already at the small table in the kitchen and not at the large one in the dining room. Three could sit at the small one, and three there were.

"Run downstairs and get you a Big K out of the fridge," encouraged Papa.

Kevin did not argue. He shuffled down the stairs, with caution, as quickly as safely possible. When he opened the refrigerator door, he found he had options. There was a knock off Mountain Dew and root beer. He grabbed the Citrus Drop. Back up the stairs, taking two at a time, he hustled. The door at the top had a large window. He shut the door a little too hard, and the window rattled.

"Now, listen here," said Nan. "You break my window, and I'm going to eat your chocolate pie without you."

He laughed. "Sorry, Nanny."

They sat and fixed their sandwiches. Simple white bread with a slice of cheese, a slice of bologna and some Miracle Whip were all Kevin required. Papa and Nanny added slices of tomato and onion to theirs.

"I might have you pick the tomatoes this afternoon," Nan suggested.

"No problem."

"Is there anything else down there that needs to be picked, Kenny?" Papa's first name was Kenneth. Everyone except his kids and grandkids called him Kenny.

Papa stroked his chin. "I don't think so, but he knows what to look for, don't you, Kev? I think I got most everything on Saturday before we left."

The afternoon was slow and relaxed. Kevin took a bucket to the garden and collected the red tomatoes. He picked a few beans. That was about it. The garden received plenty of sunlight, and the afternoon heat became uncomfortable. Kevin took the vegetables to Nan and then went down to the basement to read.

Before dinner, he helped Papa work on the log splitter. The old machine was not running well, and Papa wanted to make sure the engine would work before he really needed it.

Dinner was at the dining room table. Nan served spaghetti. Kevin loved the way she prepared it. The meat was minimal and finely ground. She added a little chili pepper for spice. He ate a plateful with a piece of garlic bread.

"I'm saving room for pie," he assured Nan.

She looked at Papa and smiled. "Oh shoot," she said, "I knew I forgot something."

"Too late, Nan. I saw it in the microwave."

Papa chuckled a deep laugh from his belly. "He's on to you, Helen. You can't fool the boy."

Nan retrieved the pie and a clean plate. She allowed Kevin to serve himself a generous slice.

The chocolate cream was topped with homemade meringue. Nan was a pro. She could have sold that pie at any restaurant. The pudding was the perfect consistency, and the meringue looked professional. While the pie sliced nicely and stood instead of spilling over, the texture was still creamy and delicious.

"You're the best, Nan."

She beamed. Something about Kevin's appreciation for the pie always made the effort worthwhile.

"I'm going to have to teach you the recipe soon. I don't know how much longer I can make 'em."

Kevin had heard this for a few years, too. Nan was eternal. Nan would never not be there to make him pie.

"If you teach me how to make your pie, I'll weigh a thousand pounds."

Nan cleaned up after dinner. Kevin slouched into a couch with a book.

For a while, Nanny and Papa attended to their routine, watching the news and putzing in the kitchen. Then, Wheel of Fortune came on the air. Kevin joined them. As letters were guessed and tiles uncovered, they took turns attempting to be the first to solve the puzzle. Kevin was getting good at figuring them out. Nanny and Papa were quick, too. They guessed a few and missed a few.

Kevin stood. "I'm going to take a shower."

"That smells like a good idea. I thought Nan left the trash can open."

Kevin smiled. Papa was always kidding. He grabbed his stuff and decided to use the basement shower instead of the upstairs bath.

When he got back to the room, Nan had already pulled the sofa cushions off and pulled out the twin bed. Nan fetched clean sheets and a blanket for him.

"Now, you don't stay up too late," she warned. "We'll probably get you up around 5:00 in the morning to work in the garden." Kevin knew that was hardly the truth.

"If you wait til five, I'll probably already be finished. Better get me up at 4." He could tease right back.

"You're on, mister. Get him up at four, Kenny."

"How much extra coffee should I make?"

"I don't drink coffee, Papa."

"It'll put hair on your chest!"

"I already got one hair. Do I need more?"

His grandparents laughed. He enjoyed their mirth. Laughter was good for the soul and his favorite way to deal with life and the things he did not want to remember.

Nan gave him a kiss and said good night. As she closed the door, Kevin spoke up, "I love you!"

"I love you, too, Kevin."

With the door closed, Kevin had options. There was a VCR, and he could watch a movie. He could turn on the television. Without his parents here, he could watch whatever he wanted, or he could read.

He opted for the television first. Using the remote, he surfed through the channels. Papa did not pay for cable or satellite. The channels were few and the shows uninteresting. He turned the power off and set the remote aside. Kevin went to the bookcase looking for something good. He opened a glass door and pulled out Sir Arthur and His Knights. This was a great one.

Before long, he was engrossed in the story of Arthur and Excalibur. The lamp next to the couch was the only light. He lay on his side and turned towards the soft glow. Above the television, a light oak-framed clock was hung. Kevin glanced over occasionally. He had started reading around 8:30 and already nearly an hour-and-a-half had passed. He was beginning to get sleepy. Closing the book, he set the tome on the same cabinet that held the lamp. He reached up and turned it off. Getting comfortable took a minute. The house was cool enough that the blanket was helpful. He liked snuggling under covers. Once he was on his side and curled in a ball under the quilt, he closed his eyes and let his imagination take him back to King Arthur's world.

He came to consciousness with a feeling of pleasure between his legs. His penis was hard, and he was thrusting his hips trying to hit that good feeling over and over. Out of nowhere, the memories of Sam came flooding in. For years, he had not allowed himself to think about those incidents. He thought of them occasionally but would never let himself dwell on what happened. Sam's family had moved to South Carolina a few months after the incident in the church bathroom. The Stephens had visited the Parks since, but Sam had never touched him again. Not like that.

But tonight, he was there. He remembered everything, and he could not stop. His own penis felt like Sam's had looked back then, stiff and throbbing. Visions of Sam using his socks to caress his penis came back to him. Kevin rolled over and found a pair of socks in his bag in the dark. Throwing off the blanket and sheets, he pulled his pajamas and underwear down and felt himself. He was dripping just like he had witnessed with the older teenager. Kevin took the socks and used his fingers to hold them together at the edges so that they gripped his penis tightly. The pleasure was intense. Kevin continued. He felt the urge to go a little faster. A new sensation came over him. He felt creamy drips on his belly. His penis flexed and then gradually went limp. Kevin felt a wave of emotions. While the sensations were amazing, he felt ashamed. Something about those times with Sam were not right, and he didn't want to think about any of it, at all, ever. But the memories were there, fresh, like the television showing his secret moments of guilt.

He cleaned himself off with the socks, dropped them on the floor and pulled his underwear and pajamas back over his hips. He needed to go to the bathroom, but he didn't want to get up. Reluctantly, he did anyway. Down the hall to the left, he made a right before running into Nanny's and Papa's door. The closet with the washer and dryer was there and then the bathroom door. The floor transitioned from carpet to linoleum. Cool tingles rippled from his soles. He shut the door and opened the toilet lid. Pulling his bottoms down, he sat on the toilet instead of standing. A minute passed before he began to pee. Even when the dripping stopped, he sat a bit longer trying to process the flood of thoughts and feelings that had just washed over him.

He knew a little bit about puberty. Sixth-grade boys have erections and don't know what to do other than laugh at each other. He thought of his friend, Travis, giggling in class, pulling his pants tight against his waist and pointing to his boner.

Kevin never said anything to anyone about the things that Sam had done to him. He felt like it was wrong and shameful. He had heard preaching, too, that said men being naked with men was evil. God judged people for that by sending them to hell. Kevin slumped on the seat and buried his face in his hands. God was going to send him to hell. He stood up and closed the lid. No need to flush and wake Nanny and Papa. He padded quietly back out the door, turned left, stepped down the hallway and ducked into his room. He shut the door quietly and got back under the covers. All he could see was Sam playing with himself and asking Kevin to touch him. He felt the pull of Sam's hand on the back of his neck pulling him to Sam's groin. He felt the pressure of Sam pushing into from behind. He could not escape the sadness, the shame, the guilt. He cried. Tears dampened his pillow, and he pled with God, "I'm sorry."

Chapter Seven

Day 5

Kevin leaned against the shower wall and let the steaming hot water rinse his body. This 5:30 AM ritual was a habit formed during his freshman year. Getting to the bathroom early allowed him to avoid most of the other young men. College life had whittled his six-foot, one inch frame to just 160 pounds. Transversing campus for chapel and classes, eating few meals and working extra hours on the weekends had removed any excess fat and left only the bones.

However, the finish line was in sight. He had survived five semesters and the sixth was halfway complete. By taking a course during the summer, he was going to eliminate an eighth semester. He would be done by December.

His whole childhood, he had dreamt of being a man on campus at Bob Jones University, but he was not prepared for life in the dorms. He enjoyed elements of the camaraderie. His first roommates were a Korean high schooler named Jacob and a senior named Joe. Jacob was a good kid. He studied hard. Popular with the other Korean students, the room was often full of visitors. They liked Kevin and Joe because they shared food with them and kidded them when they spoke Korean.

Kevin's introduction to Joe had come through his sister who was also on campus that year. She graduated two years earlier but remained on staff. Her former roommate and best friend was Amy. Amy's brother was Joe. The two sisters thought their brothers would enjoy being roommates because they had similar sardonic personalities. The sisters were not wrong.

While Kevin did not mind his roommates, dorm life afforded little privacy. Constant male presence caused triggers in his psyche that Kevin did not yet fully grasp, but he felt them deeply.

Kevin spent one semester in the room with Joe and Jacob. Then Joe promoted him to a minor leadership position down the hall. That was his parallel progression in college. As he was taking classes and completing academic work, he was also being promoted to leadership on the social side.

This semester was his second as hall leader. He was responsible for a wing of dorm rooms and the sixty guys who lived in them. His duties included rule enforcement, spiritual accountability and social engagement. Well-liked by the young men on his hall and the other hall leaders, Kevin had the reputation for being tough but fair. When warranted, Kevin could confront rule-breakers and write demerits as easily as anyone. However, he preferred to ask questions, understand people and help solve problems. Demerits never helped a man improve. They only demonstrated where he was lacking or where the institution thought he was wrong. Other hall leaders and dorm supervisors enjoyed Kevin, too. His wry humor and dry wit often brought levity to otherwise boring meetings. Even the Dean of Men knew the name Kevin Stephens, though everyone called him solely by his last name.

This would be his last semester as hall leader. Next semester, for the first time, he was taking a demotion so that he could work a better-paying job off campus. His role would still have some leadership requirements, but he would only oversee a few rooms instead of an entire hall, and there would be no remuneration. As the end of his college life began to dip below the horizon, he was planning a new dawn beyond. He could not wait to live without male roommates.

For the past two years, he had been dating. Tiffany was her name – not to be confused with his sister. But she was named for his sister. Her parents, Dan and Rachel, were old friends of his parents. And guess where their paths crossed? They met in Greenville, South Carolina because of Bob Jones University.

Bob Jones University had been a central theme in Kevin's life since before he was born. The private, Christian college in Greenville, South Carolina had shaped their family for years.

Mom and Dad graduated from Fairmont State University in West Virginia. During college, they were married, and they became serious about church. Dad had not even been a Christian when he met Mom. His come-to-Jesus moment happened at her church when Dad was a young adult. Nanny and Papa still attended little Isaac Creek Baptist, and Kevin had been there many times.

In Fairmont, Dad and Mom got involved with an independent, Baptist church – independent because the church did not belong to any denomination. The pastor and his wife encouraged Kevin's parents to participate in church life, and they did.

The longer Dad was active with the group of believers, the more he wished he had a greater knowledge of the Bible. He was not raised in church. His major in college was business administration. After some deliberation and consultation, Dad and Mom decided to move to Greenville. Mom would take employment as a nurse, and Dad would get a master's degree in religion so that he could be a better Sunday school teacher.

They found an apartment to rent on East North Street just off campus. The apartment was part of a large white house. The landlord rented the top floor as a unit and split the downstairs into two additional units. Dad and Mom lived in the upper level. As the semesters passed, they formed some long-lasting friendships with some of their downstairs neighbors. One of those young married couples was Dan and Rachel Johnson.

Mom gave birth to a daughter in Greenville. The new parents named her Tiffany. Dan and Rachel would hear that name often and sometimes play with Tiffany into her toddler years. When they later moved to Milwaukee and had a daughter of their own, they also chose the name Tiffany.

Two more children were born to Dan and Rachel: another daughter, Savannah, and a son, Jon. After several years in Milwaukee, Dan took his family on the road to preach in churches all around the United States. They lived in an RV for nearly eight years. During that time, they made several stops in Glenford and reconnected with the Stephens. Kevin still remembered the first time he met Tiffany. Her ninth birthday was that week on September 1st. With party hats atop their heads and kazoos hanging off their lips, they wished her a happy birthday and enjoyed homemade ice cream cake, a Johnson tradition.

Kevin thought she was cute. He finagled his way next to her at every chance. With Savannah, they rode bikes down country back roads and explored the old train tracks that led directly from the church to town. An old trestle still crossed Jonathan Creek deep in the woods. Here, Kevin made a glorious blunder attempting to impress. The Johnsons had a poodle mix named Angel that often tagged along with them. Laying their bikes down by the trail, the three explorers ambled their way to the creek bed under the short bridge. Mud along the stream was thin. Kevin detected a line of tracks. "Hey, look!" Tiffany and

Savannah surrounded him and stared at the tracks. "Raccoon prints," Kevin announced with authority. For a few moments, the trio stared at the evidence of the creature's passing. Then Savannah disagreed. "Those are Angel's tracks." Down the creek side, Angel came loping. All three of them laughed, but Kevin was embarrassed. "What a dumb mistake," he thought to himself. This became a running joke for a while. Kevin had failed to astound his friends with his woodland expertise.

With each visit, the two were changing, morphing from children into pre-adolescents into teens. They occasionally crossed paths elsewhere as during the summer between Kevin's 7th and 8th grade years. He attended Science Camp at Bob Jones, and Tiffany attended Music Camp during the same week. On the large campus, they saw each other occasionally at meals in the spacious dining hall.

The Johnsons quit traveling just before Tiffany's junior year of high school. When Dan and Rachel brought their family to Glenford for the last time before starting a church in Franklin, Tennessee, Tiffany was fifteen. She was beautiful. Brown, curly hair framed her smiling face. Her cheeks were full, and she had bright green eyes. Kevin was smitten. The guys at church teased him.

"You're going to marry her."

"No, I'm not," Kevin protested. "She doesn't even like me that much."

Tiffany was more reserved towards him now that she was a young lady. That visit, she spent more time with Kevin's sister, and Kevin spent more time with her sister. Savannah was just thirteen and still more than willing to ride bikes and have fun.

For a few years, Kevin would only hear rumors of what was transpiring in Tiffany's life. Her dad started the new church in the

Nashville suburb. Tiffany was involved. She was finishing high school. She graduated. She was going to attend Bob Jones.

Arriving on campus a full year before Kevin, Tiffany adapted easily. Her mother's parents lived just off campus. Dr. Abelman had once been a teacher in the university's school of religion passing on the wisdom gleaned from years of pastoring to young men wanting to enter the ministry. Grandmother Abelman kept a fastidious, simple home and cooked delicious southern meals. Kevin later swore she added pecans to every dish and even the iced tea. Tiffany had a place to escape the chaos of the dorm.

She was asked out frequently and went to meals and events with various young men, many of whom she had met during her family's travels. Academic success was important to her, and she studied hard. She also had a few cousins that were on campus. They were close. Relatives of the university president, they were a dangerous club. They gossiped about their various dates and kept each other informed regarding eligible bachelors and BMOC's (Big Men On Campus).

Kevin was oblivious to these connections when he landed on campus during her sophomore year. They reconnected quickly because Tiffany, his sister, chauffeured Tiffany Johnson to off-campus church on Sunday nights. As a member of the faculty, Kevin's sister was an approved chaperone and could take a mixed group in her personal vehicle. She drove. Kevin sat in the passenger seat. Tiffany J. filled the back seat with friends and family. As he steadily met the several cousins, Kevin sensed their scrutiny. Kevin and Tiffany were often side-by-side at church. Kevin was a consummate Christian gentleman. He held the hymnal for her. Before and after church, they chatted. Sometimes Kevin made snarky comments to her quietly during the preaching. If he could get her to smile, he considered that a win. If he could make her laugh, he would be ecstatic. That was the goal, to get her to completely break out of that demure, fundamentalist, good-girl solemnity. She liked him. He knew it. They had a lot in common. Still, he did not ask her out directly until the end of the year.

He went on few dates that freshman year. For one, he was busy. While he took a light academic load his first semester to get adjusted, he compensated with a maximum academic schedule during the second half of the year. Both semesters, he worked on and off campus. He was also shy. Tiffany J. was dating other guys anyway. He was content to be friends and not take the risk of being direct just yet. The last major event on the spring calendar was a concert with the Canadian Brass. Artist Series was a BJU tradition. Twice a school year, the university hosted a well-known classical artist or group. Kevin was especially excited for this one. Canadian Brass was a personal favorite. As a fellow trumpeter, he was eager to hear the best.

Social engagement between the sexes was closely monitored. However, the college facilitated communication from the women's side of campus to the men's in a couple of ways. Every dorm room had a telephone. Before widespread access to cell phones, the landline provided an indispensable connection. Calling the opposite dorms was easy. Four-digit codes were all that was required to ring another dorm room. All the girl's dorm room codes began with the same number as did the men's albeit with a varied digit. Kevin could pick up the phone, punch in the number four and then add three additional digits that connected to a specific dorm on the women's side. He knew his sister's code by heart. He had also discovered the room code for Tiffany J.

This simple system was ripe for abuse. One of the funniest moments of his freshman year was learning a popular prank from one of the veteran students.

"Hey, Stephens, watch this." Greg pulled Kevin into his room and picked up the line. He dialed a random number on the girl's side of campus.

"Hello," a female voice answered.

"Uh, hey," said Greg. "I need to ask you something. Oh wait, sorry, can you hold on for a second?"

The unsuspecting girl answered, "Sure."

Greg tapped the plunger for a three-way call and quickly dialed a random guy's dorm. Sure enough, someone picked up.

"Yeah, it's Tim."

Greg said nothing but tapped the switch to add the young lady into the conversation.

Tim got impatient with the silence. "Hello?" he said belying his annoyance.

"Yes."

"Who is this?" Tim wanted to know.

"Who are you looking for?"

"I'm not looking for anyone. Who are you looking for? You called me." Tim was slightly exasperated.

"No, I didn't. You called me." She was getting annoyed too.

Greg covered the receiver and snickered. Kevin was chuckling, too. This was great.

"I don't know what you're talking about."

"Listen," she snapped. "If you call a girl up, you should be ready to talk to her." And she slammed the phone.

Tim sighed and also hung up.

The pranksters burst into laughter.

Additionally, every dormitory had a box in the lobby. That box was divided into five compartments each labeled with the different names of the women's dorms. The women had a corresponding box in the lobby with the five different names of the men's dorms. A letter could be addressed to a specific dorm room and dropped into the box any time during the day. At 10:00 PM, the notes would be collected and delivered to the corresponding dormitory. The hall leaders would grab the notes and set them on a table in the middle of the hall. Students would walk down to see if anyone had sent a letter to them.

Kevin wrote an invitation to Tiffany asking her to attend the Canadian Brass concert with him. Dropping the note into the box, he waited for a reply. A few nights later, he received a response in the affirmative. Their first official date was scheduled. He made a couple of calls before the anticipated night just to make sure all the details were set. Those quick calls of confirmation turned into hours of conversation.

Twigs was a fancy floral shop near the Haywood Mall. Kevin borrowed his sister's car the day of the concert and went shopping. He ordered a large bouquet of stargazer lilies and red roses. Tiffany J. was delighted.

Artist Series performances were usually held in the gigantic Founder's Memorial Amphitorium. An enormous venue for such a small campus, the arena seated about seven thousand people. Tickets were sold not only to students but to visitors as well. Every seat was packed for the Canadian Brass. They delivered a show that made Kevin want to practice his own trumpet a bit harder. Every moment with Tiffany was a welcome break from the pressure he felt in the dorms. Her feminine charm was a delightful contrast. Kevin had male friends, but he liked the females better. After the concert, he accompanied her back to her dorm entrance. They made plans to rendezvous at the campus coffee shop before summer break.

Normally, they would have passed the entire summer without seeing each other. But this summer was extraordinary. Tiffany Stephens was getting married. Her suitor was a young man from Milwaukee. His parents were first-generation immigrants from Germany. The family name was Schneider. New to Wisconsin many years before, they were introduced to a young pastor and began attending his new church. That pastor was Dan Johnson.

Karl Schneider was their youngest son. He had graduated from Bob Jones and started his career as a financial analyst a couple of years before Tiffany Stephens graduated. Through introductions, he met Dad and found out more about the Stephens family. He saw pictures of Tiffany and asked to meet her. Their courtship had been simple and short.

Kevin was largely oblivious to their romantic machinations. The previous summer, he had spent twelve weeks traveling the east coast helping with a community youth outreach event for churches called The War. The little he knew about his sister's romantic life occurred by accident. On Valentine's Day, he had sent her a red rose with a little note. Over the years, he had shown his sister love in simple ways. He took the gesture for granted. For her part, her little brother's act of love and kindness was bitterly received. When she saw the rose, she assumed her fiancé was responsible for the gift. When she discovered that he had instead done nothing to observe the romantic holiday, she cried. Karl had a lot to learn.

Karl and Tiffany planned a large wedding. Included in the details was an invitation to Karl's former pastor to be part of the ceremony. The Johnsons would be attending.

Kevin spent that summer working for a transportation company in Columbus. This was his second summer at the business, and he was responsible for prepping and painting semi-trucks and trailers. Days were long because of the fifty-minute commute. The return trip in the afternoon was often longer because of heavy traffic. Busy with his own responsibilities, he did little to contribute to the wedding efforts. He did attend the wedding. And he spent some time with Tiffany J.

Sis moved to Milwaukee with Karl, and Kevin went back to Bob Jones. Kevin and Tiffany J. began to spend more time together. Sunday evenings were still spent at church, but they no longer had the luxury of riding with his sister. They switched churches and took a bus. Many of the local churches sent transportation to campus so that students could attend. Many students stayed in the dorms which was permitted. While the Sunday morning service on campus was mandatory, evening services were optional. Kevin and Tiffany rarely missed, however. Both sets of parents expected them to continue church attendance and involvement. And both of them wanted to go. Being together was an additional incentive. After visiting quite a few churches, they began to primarily attend Fellowship Baptist Church in nearby Taylors.

The two had grown close, and now they were beginning to discuss their future together after graduation. Tiffany was graduating in May. Kevin would finish in December. March was already here. Soon, Kevin wanted to propose. He was saving for a diamond.

But this morning, standing in the shower, he was in angst. Bob Jones did not have a typical spring break. There were no vacations, no trips by students to Myrtle Beach or Daytona. Instead, they reserved one week in March every year at the midpoint of the semester for an event called Bible Conference. Every day had multiple preaching services which students were required to attend. Kevin was unfazed by this. He had sat through more services at this point in his life than most people attended in an eighty-year lifespan.

He and Tiffany spent a lot of time together. And he felt that he needed to unburden his soul. For weeks, the internal pressure had been mounting. If he was going to ask Tiffany to marry him, he needed to be transparent with her regarding his sexual history. She deserved to know that he was not a virgin, per se. Keeping his sexual assault from her was not fair, if he intended to keep pursuing a long-term relationship. And such was his intent.

She was about to wrap up her college tenure. Her major was TESL – Teaching English as a Second Language. An excellent student, she was also a hall leader. Academic and leadership responsibilities had kept both of them busy. They found times to connect through each week over meals and between classes. Some evenings were spent studying together in the social area at the extremely conservative university. Known as "The Dating Parlor," a chaperone patrolled the large room keeping an eye on the numerous couples. Like a library, whispers were preferred. Couples shared love seats in the dimly lit room but were not permitted to touch each other. The chaperone could write demerits for infractions and even ask students to leave.

Kevin and Tiffany knew the chaperones. Tiffany had once held that position. Plus, as hall leaders and older students, they were known to many. On the small couch, Tiffany would diligently accomplish assignments. Kevin rarely had outstanding projects. School had always been relatively easy for him. He was not going to graduate with honors. He would barely miss with a 3.4 GPA. But he did well without committing to a lot of extra study time. Once he heard the material covered in class or completed a reading, his retention was good enough to pass most quizzes and tests with at least eighty percent. His time out of class was spent working both on and off campus. On Saturdays, he took jobs in town with local residents and would help with landscaping projects. Paid in cash, he used the money for his incidentals and to keep Tiffany readily supplied with cappuccinos from the campus coffee shop.

Those nights on the campus couch, under the watchful eyes of the university chaperone, Kevin would alternately help Tiffany with her work and make her laugh. And when she found a good stopping place for the night, they would pull out The Count of Monte Cristo and read to each other.

Kevin was sure they were getting married. Their destiny had been foreshadowed from childhood. But this burden of sexual trauma haunted him. He needed to tell her. He needed to know she would love him regardless, or they needed to break up.

Turning the water off, he slipped a hand past the curtain and grabbed his towel. He wrapped the large navy cloth around his waist, pulled the curtain aside and stepped into his sandals. His mind had become increasingly bothered by his relationship. "Am I good enough for her? Should I get married? Will she be disappointed or disgusted? Will she think I'm a pervert? Will I become an abuser, too? Am I safe?" Heavy thoughts for a twenty-one-year-old young man. But most of these questions had dogged him for years.

His room was still dark. He had already prepared his clothing for the day. Dressing in the dark was second nature. Roommates always appreciated his commitment to stealth during the early hours. Underwear, pants, t-shirt and socks. This was good enough to begin the day. Another hour remained before his responsibilities began. Needing more time to think, he grabbed his Bible, a journal and a pen and slipped back out the door. Down the hallway to the main stairs, he trotted down a few flights to the basement. Every dorm had a prayer room. Tucked in the basement, the room was empty of furniture. On all sides there was a padded bench permanently installed as a feature. Few men were ever down here. When Kevin entered, one other hall leader was hunched over his Bible. Kevin went to the opposite corner. He knelt on the floor and opened his Bible. Reading without comprehension, he was still mulling over a potential conversation with Tiffany about his childhood sexual assault. He opened his journal and wrote a few lines of prayer. Guilt. That's what he felt. This weight had nearly crushed him before.

Following puberty and the discovery of his own sexuality, Kevin was increasingly sensitive to the mentions of sex in the sermons he heard. Most preachers only mentioned sexual sin in passing, and Kevin never remembered any nuanced discussion of how to handle sex as a victim. In fact, the overwhelming majority seemed uncomfortable with even the positive treatment of marital sex. A few speakers had randomly spoken against masturbation but without any clear use of scripture.

Kevin masturbated frequently. He enjoyed the pleasure. This caused further anxiety. "Is masturbation sin? Why does this feel so good, if it's so wrong? Do other people masturbate? Do godly men masturbate?"

His thoughts were muddled with memories.

During his freshman year, the word "wuss" was commonly used in the dormitory as an insult to guy's machoism. Kevin used the term, too, never really thinking about its etymology. This epithet became known by the Dean of Men who conducted a hall meeting to address his concerns.

All of the men on every hallway in each men's dormitory were required to sit in the hall and listen to a broadcast of the dean's remarks. He addressed them live over the sound system.

"Men, it has come to my attention that a term is being used that is inappropriate for a Christian. The word is..." and he paused awkwardly, "wa...oos." Everyone chuckled. Unfortunately, he was not finished. "You may not know this, but that word is a reference to a female's Gen...uh Gen...Gentile," he finally uttered assertively then caught his error, "...er, genitalia." Again, laughter up and down the halls. The old geezer was struggling. Kevin was still confused regarding the connection between "wuss" and vagina. "Men, I do not want to hear this word on our Christian campus. We must be respectful of women and each other. I am asking the hall leaders to warn those who use the term and to issue demerits to repeat offenders. Swearing and vulgar language will not be tolerated by Bob Jones University. Let's honor God with our words." Needless to say, the uncomfortable public address only made the word explode in popularity, although its use paled in comparison to a new popular euphemism: "You lady's Gentile" became a slanderous and humorous pejorative.

Dad had attempted his own talk about sex with his son going into adolescence.

Kevin thought of that conversation from time to time. Dad had brought him into his pastoral study.

"Have a seat," he instructed his twelve-year-old.

Kevin hopped into the old banker's chair – dark-stained wood wrapped in leather on the arms, the same leather attached by brass rivets to the back of the seat, a thin leather cushion barely padding the seat.

Dad sat in his comfortable office chair of powder blue cloth. He leaned forward, hands folded together, with his arms resting on the large oak desk.

"I want to talk to you about something very important." He launched into an analogy that involved nature references. Kevin checked out mentally. If only his dad knew what he knew. Compartmentalizing the discussion with Dad, Kevin nodded and feigned attention while battling internal nerves. He felt terrible. He had already had sex, so he thought.

Dad wrapped up his comments by asking Kevin, "Will you promise to be pure until you get married?"

Kevin nodded while simultaneous thoughts ran through his mind:"It's too late," and, "No girl will ever want to kiss me anyway."

Time had proven that would not be an issue. Girls liked him. They wanted to kiss.

A sermon in chapel during his senior year was also memorable. The preacher began by handing a rose to the junior high students on the front row and asked that they pass the dainty flower through the entire assembly. In the meantime, he lectured regarding moral purity. Using scripture, he announced that all sexual activity outside of marriage was sin including masturbation. By the time the pale blossom reached the senior class, few petals remained and the plant was faded and shriveled. He retrieved the illustration and held it before the teenagers. Then he held up another rose, still fresh. "Which rose would you rather receive?" Kevin was sick to the point of nausea. He was not an untouched rose.

Time after time, he heard words of condemnation without any words of comfort for wounded souls. He felt targeted by God, the only impure sinner in his pure, Christian world. Other sinners that were discovered were removed from service and often left the church. He was stuck. Only he knew that he did not deserve to be serving God. And he was serving a lot. He led music and preached at the nursing home. He taught children's church. He was a participant in the Christmas cantatas. He sang solos and duets and was a crucial member of the choir. He played his trumpet for the congregation. He led youth group prayers. He accompanied deacons on visitation on Tuesday nights. He was at the men's prayer breakfasts. Only his immediate family were more involved in ministry than he was. But he was the dirty one, the sinner, the outsider.

He had attended the Wilds Christian Camp in Brevard, North Carolina during the same summer when he commenced puberty at Nan's and Papa's. Some of the preaching had been especially censorious of premarital sex and homosexuality. On the last night, Kevin was so miserable that he went forward to confess. He could not bring himself to tell the male counselor anything other than that he needed God's forgiveness. He recommitted his life to God. A panacea at best, the measure helped a bit.

Yet here he was again, begging God for pardon and absolution.32 He feared that his hands were covered in soot, and that if he touched Tiffany, she would be dirty, too.

The morning bell roused him from his spiritual torpor. Determined that today would be the day he came clean with his girlfriend, he got up and attended to his duties.

Three sessions would be held that day, and during the interludes, Kevin and Tiffany would talk, meet up with friends and eat meals at the dining common. You could never guess who would cross your path at Bible Conference. Kevin knew hundreds of missionaries, evangelists, pastors and Bob Jones alumni. This week was a family reunion of sorts.

Kevin finished his last responsibility before heading to the first service. Making sure that every room was vacant, he met up with Ian, his counterpart from the opposite hall.

"Who's the speaker this morning?" Ian was gung-ho about Bible Conference. Ian was enthusiastic about everything.

"Hey, man! Dr. Minnick is preaching this morning. This is going to be great!"

Mark Minnick was the pastor of the church Kevin had attended with Tiffany J. and his sister during his freshman year. He was also a professor on campus. Kevin had listened to him many times. So had Ian.

"I was hoping for someone I hadn't heard before," Kevin offered truthfully.

"Yeah, it's hit or miss. I never heard the missionary that spoke last night, and I won't mind never listening to him again."

Studying for ministry had turned them into harsh critics. Actually, being a preacher's kid had turned Kevin into the Ebert of sermon evaluation.

"We can be sure Minnick will exegete the scriptures." That was important. Entertainment was not as important as exposition. They wanted to learn something. Few preachers were that interesting anyway.

Truth was, Kevin learned the most from his own study. He rarely learned anything new from a sermon or a Bible class. At this point, he was capable of doing his own research and drawing his own conclusions. He found that quite a few speakers did not preach from the Bible so much as they used the old book as an excuse for their own personal pet peeves.

Kevin had become increasingly resentful of the politics of Bible Conference, too. Dad had never been asked to speak, and he was a better preacher than many of the men who came from large churches. Kevin valued the humility and authenticity of men like Dad. They seemed to be few.

"Well, hopefully, he's preaching something we have not heard before," he said to Ian as they parted ways, meaning he did not want to hear a sermon Minnick had already preached.

Tiffany was already waiting by the side entrance they typically used.

"Good morning, Chickadee."

She smiled. Her nickname stemmed from some beautiful note cards that Kevin often used for her.

Meetings were awkward. There was none of the normal physical affection associated with a healthy relationship. He could not give her a brief hug, a peck on the cheek or even squeeze her hand. They just stood there looking into each other's eyes surrounded by other young adults behaving the same goofy way.

They turned and entered the building through a side door. Kevin was still awed by the magnificent auditorium. He felt naked, like he was being watched. He liked back rows and side aisles. Today, they had entered late enough that the ushers were sending them backwards.

An occasional, "Stephens!" would erupt from the chaos as Kevin was greeted by students in passing. He was popular. He did not know why. Guys were not shy about yelling to him in public. He was slightly embarrassed. He was trying to go unnoticed.

Tiffany had experienced this with him many times. She was drawn to his shy confidence, his humble bravado. He was a complex human being: a proportionate mix of intelligence, humility, confidence, sarcasm, thoughtfulness and spirituality. He was sensitive and empathic. He was mischievous and contrarian. And he was good-looking. Her chief complaint was that he was thin to the point of appearing sickly. He needed to put on a few pounds. She got him to her grandmother's dining room for home cooking as often as possible. Still, he looked like a marathon runner with a tapeworm.

Ushers escorted them into a row near the middle of the auditorium but off to the right side. They shuffled the narrow row to their seats. Kevin was always nervous that he would need to pee and have to cause a kerfuffle to escape to the bathroom. Leaving a service prematurely was a no-no. Mom had been his pew companion for most of his life. She had denied every request to leave the pew before the service ended.

Only when he was a teenager would he occasionally be allowed to sit anywhere other than the front second pew beside Mother. If there were any shenanigans, he would immediately lose the privilege.

He sat beside Tiffany in the theater-style seats and checked his bladder. He should be good. His long legs were constrained by the space, and his knees occasionally bumped Tiffany's leg.

He whispered, "Pardon my indiscretion. I hope that the caress of my knee does not lead you into temptation."

She laughed out loud and hard. "Why, sir, your knee is indeed tempting me but not to impurity. I want to smack you because it's annoying."

He chuckled. "That's what every guy wants to hear. I want you to know that I like you enough to annoy you forever."

"Wow. That's beyond romantic. Please, be my constant companion and irritation."

"Sounds like an average marriage actually."

"Are you proposing, Sir?" She resumed a Jane Eyre comportment.

"When I ask you to marry me, neither of us will know it," he assured her. "I'm not that smooth."

"Non sequitur is your expertise. I'll probably assume you're proposing when you're actually just tying your shoe."

"That sounds about right," he agreed. "Just when you think I'm going to zig, that's when I...get a pizza."

A call to stand for the opening hymn interrupted their banter. Three hymns, a prayer, an offering and a special sacred performance preceded every sermon. They denounced the Catholics but had an equally predictable and boring liturgy.

Kevin's interest in the sermon varied from speaker to speaker. Sometimes he took notes. Often, he stared while retreating to his imagination. Dr. Minnick delivered sermons that usually warranted notes. His insights were keen and his applications clear.

Still, as good as the sermon might be, Kevin was occupied with his thoughts from the morning and his impending discussion with Tiffany. His stomach churned. He was so distraught that his belly audibly groaned.

Tiffany leaned towards him. "Wow. Did you not eat breakfast?" She whispered.

"Nope," he admitted.

She shook her head and resumed paying attention. She, too, was the veteran of a million sermons. Her knowledge of the Bible was as broad as his own, perhaps broader. She had a two-month head start, after all.

As the service drew to a close, the congregation rose for a final hymn. Every amen was a starter's pistol for the exits. Kevin abhorred the rush. They sat back down and waited for the aisles to clear.

"Why didn't you eat breakfast?" Tiffany chided.

"I had other things on my mind," he admitted. "Let's get lunch at the snack shop."

That idea was met with enthusiasm.

"Wait," he hesitated. "What's on the menu for lunch?"

"We're not missing out on anything good," she assured him. "I checked this morning. I can't remember because it was forgettable."

"Okay, snack shop it is. We can eat outside."

The lawns were strictly off limits throughout the school year with the lone exception of Bible Conference. Generally, the weather was spring in Greenville which meant bright skies, comfortable temperatures and the constant threat that the day would turn to rain. Today was blue skies and seventy degrees, perfect conditions for finding a spot outdoors.

As the building cleared, they joined the straggling exit and made their way up a slight incline towards the Student Center. They pivoted at the corner into the atrium between the buildings that held the game room and dating parlor on the left and the snack shop, coffee shop and bookstore on the right. The line was long for the snack shop, but waiting was a given during Bible Conference. They joined the queue.

Kevin turned to Tiffany as a thought dawned on him, "This is your last Bible Conference." His eyes widened. "This is my last Bible Conference!"

She laughed. "Yeah, I guess you're right." Her thoughts churned. "I'm not going to miss it."

"Good news. You'll be able to come back, if you do."

"Can you imagine? Maybe for a service or a reunion, but no, I'm never sitting through twenty-seven services in six days again."

"What if I was speaking?"

"Just send me the notes."

Tiffany had never heard him preach. "Are you dreadfully boring?"

"Well, some say it's the best nap they've ever taken, and sleep is a gift. To be fair, that was at the nursing home, and they did not need much encouragement."

"That's a pretty forgiving audience. What about when you speak to a group of living people?"

"Sometimes they stay awake. I have an exposition of Psalm 119 that only takes about five hours."

"Seems rushed."

"You're an evangelist's daughter. You're used to preaching that's over in twenty minutes."

"True. If the sermon has more than three alliterated points and two jokes, you're not doing it right."

"I'll let you write my sermons."

"Ooh, I could do that. Now I'm intrigued."

"You know your mom is a better speaker than your dad."

She laughed. "She's more popular with ladies' retreat than he is with men's."

"So, she's been writing his sermons the whole time. Is that it?"

"Probably," Tiffany nodded, "probably."

They ordered burgers, fries and drinks and moved to the pickup line. The orders were coming through quickly. Within minutes, they had their food and moved outside looking for an empty bench. They found one that was not already occupied by young lovers staring into each other's eyes.

"Thanks for lunch."

"Hey, it only cost me three hours of spreading pine straw. You're welcome."

Talk ebbed as they bit into their burgers. Kevin lost his appetite.

"Hey, there's something I need to tell you. I love you, and I hope we can have a life together. But," he hesitated, "I need to tell you something I've never told anyone. It's really been bothering me."

Tiffany put her food down, too.

He couldn't look her in the eye. That was unusual. He was visibly uncomfortable.

She waited, then offered, "It's okay, Kevin. You can tell me." She did not know what to expect.

"When I was a kid, one of the guys in the church abused me."

"Like, how?" She wasn't sure what to say.

"He," Kevin was emotional but holding it inside, "he masturbated with me, and...stuff." He couldn't bring himself to give any more detail.

He looked up. Her face was sad and thoughtful. She was quiet for a bit.

"I'm sorry, Kevin. I don't know what to say. But I love you. It doesn't change how I feel about you."

Kevin picked up a fry. Tiffany took another bite of burger. Each retreated to their own thoughts.

Kevin gave up on his meal. He stared at the grass.

"You've never told anyone?"

"No."

"I appreciate that you told me. I do. But you really need to talk to someone who can help you. I don't know how. Maybe you should tell your parents."

He uttered the longest sigh he had ever sighed. "Yeah."

"Why wouldn't you tell them?"

Kevin shook his head. "For a lot of reasons."

"I know you'll do the right thing. Do you mind if I tell my parents?"

"No. That's fine."

Kevin's brain was foggy. He knew the next step was to talk to his parents. And he was not ready.

"Thank you," he whispered to Tiffany. "Let's go back for milkshakes."

They threw the remnants of lunch into the nearest trash receptacle and retraced their steps to the snack shop. Seeing friends at a table, they joined them and enjoyed the rest of the interlude between services.

They parted ways once the afternoon session ended. Both had leadership responsibilities on their halls. And Kevin had a phone call to make. He did not. Instead, he left campus with a couple of hall leader buddies to grab dinner. Tiffany was working through the evening session, so Kevin went with the all-male squad.

Kevin was jotting notes in his journal while a missionary talked about his experiences in Eastern Europe and discussed the necessity of faith. Kevin's notes were unrelated. His mind was preoccupied with what to say to his father. He was definitely going to speak to Dad.

Around 8:30 in the evening, the building emptied once more. Again, Kevin was among the last to leave. He had nothing scheduled until 10:30. This window afforded him the opportunity to call home. Pacing back to his dorm with reluctant steps, he hoped that a room-mate would be using the phone, or the room would be too noisy – any excuse to delay the dreaded conversation.

His room was empty. On the wall, the phone was available. He changed clothes and dialed the house in Glenford. Maybe his parents were not home...Dad picked up the line.

"Hello, Stephens' residence. Pastor speaking."

"It's me, Dad."

"Oh, hey, Kevin. How's Bible Conference?"

"Eh, it's fine."

"Any interesting speakers, so far?"

"Not really." Kevin was rarely verbose when calling his parents. Tonight, he was not anxious to engage in any conversation, let alone small talk. He decided to rip off the Band-Aid.

"Dad, I told Tiffany something today, and I need to tell you."

This was not the time for pauses, but Kevin let tension fill the space. Dad waited.

"Um, I never told anyone this, but when I was a kid, one of the teens abused me."

A sharp inhalation of breath was audible over the line.

"You're kidding me," Dad muttered, not in disbelief of Kevin but in shock at the revelation. "Who was it?" His voice was soft but stern as he managed his emotions.

The silence was long. "Sam Parks."

"You're kidding me," he repeated more slowly. "When did this happen?"

"One time at his house and one time at the church, that I remember." Kevin's own emotions were spilling into his voice.

Silence.

In the background, Mom asked, "What is it?"

"I'll tell you in a minute," Dad answered.

Dad was searching for words. "Why do you think he did that?"

"I don't know."

"I don't know what to say, son. I'm sorry. Why didn't you tell us sooner?"

"For a lot of reasons," Kevin replied, and he lost control of his tears and sobbed.

"Are you okay?"

He caught himself. "I'll be fine, Dad."

"Okay, son. I need to tell your mother. I'll call you back in a bit. Will you be up?"

"You can catch me before 10:30," Kevin assured him.

"I love you, Kevin."

"I love you, too, Dad."

The line went dead. Kevin hung up the phone and went to his bed. He was glad no one was in the room. He sobbed silently, but the convulsions would have given him away. Time lost meaning, but for a long while, he lay there, exhausted. He expected relief. Instead, there was continued uncertainty and anxiety regarding the future.

He looked at his watch. 10:00 was near. He forced himself to get up and rinse his face. Pulling a baseball cap over his eyes, he made a quick call to Tiffany.

"Hey, Chickadee, I told my dad."

"Are you okay?"

"I'll be fine. Dad's calling back soon. I just wanted to say hi. I love you."

"I love you, too. Yeah, I called my parents, too. They feel bad. They love you. Dad said if you needed to talk, you could call him."

"Thanks. Are we meeting for the morning service?"

"Yes."

"Great. I'll see you in the morning. Good night."

"Good night."

He paced the room. He really did not know how his parents would be able to help. This had taken place nearly thirteen years ago. What could be done?

With a few minutes to spare before the 10:25 PM bell, the phone rang. Just as he answered, a roommate entered. Kevin walked out into the hallway and shut the door behind him, the long cord running underneath. The hallway was busy, and no one was paying attention. He sat against the wall.

"Hey, Dad."

"Are you okay?" Dad asked again.

"I'll be fine."

"What does that mean?"

"I don't know. I'll keep doing what I've been doing." Kevin was accustomed to the burden. He could be no more specific.

Dad went silent attempting to process what that meant.

"We're coming down."

"You don't need to do that," Kevin protested.

"We're coming down," his father reiterated.

"Okay." Kevin wasn't sure where this was going or how this would be helpful.

"I've been making some calls. We'll see you tomorrow or the next. I'll let you know."

"Okay."

"I love you, son. We want to be there to support you."

"Thanks." Kevin wasn't sure what support even looked like.

"We love you, Kevin."

"Love you, too."

Once again, the line went still. Kevin stood and opened the door, reached inside and hung up the phone. Closing the door from the outside, he wandered down the hallway talking to the guys, ignoring the cauldron of emotions within.

Going through the motions, he conducted prayer meeting, made sure the hall was quiet and the lights were out. He said good night to Ian and checked the schedule for the next day. Getting in bed was the last thing he wanted. He knew what was coming. He had experienced many nights like this before. In the dark, in the quiet, the feelings and the thoughts were difficult to ignore. Sleep would come but with difficulty and after much sorrow. And who knew what forms his dreams would take.

There was nowhere else to go. He turned to walk back down the hallway and saw the note on the desk addressed to him. Chickadee.

On the notes they exchanged, they would draw a simple stick bird. He picked up the envelope and opened the card inside.

"I'm so proud of you. Love, Tiffany."

Chapter Eight

Day 6

Day broke with early sun. This would not last, Kevin believed, as he looked at the forecast. Rain would move through the area that evening. His wedding day would be sun followed by clouds, an ominous sign in retrospect. On that morning, however, his spirits were as bright as they had been in a long time.

He awakened alone in a guest room. Kevin and Tiffany had not yet slept together. The purity culture in which they had been raised frowned on even hand holding and kissing before marriage. They had not been that reserved, but the bit of petting and making out they had enjoyed had resulted in guilt. Still, they were virgins looking forward to the consummation of their love and desire for each other. Kevin had read several books regarding marriage and sex as had Tiffany. They were ready, they believed. Tonight would be their first night of lovemaking. Kevin smiled at the thought. He had waited for this. He wanted to be an amazing lover. When masturbating, he had practiced exercises of delayed gratification. Make sure she was satisfied first was the clear instruction he had gleaned from the books. He had no idea what her satisfaction would look like. The books gave some broad expectations, but the female orgasm was not as visible as the male.

Surely Tiffany would understand her body like he understood his own.

Kevin was not in a hurry to get up. His former roommate, best friend and now groomsman, Barkley, was in the next room. They were guests of a family that attended the Baptist church pastored by Tiffany's father, Dan. The new sanctuary where the young church met would host the Johnson-Stephens wedding that evening. For now, Kevin was alone.

Change was transpiring quickly. He had just finished college in December. Looking for a place to rent, his dad informed him that Art Parks had a small rental he was willing to let Kevin lease on a monthly basis.

The Parks and Stephens had survived Kevin's confession. Much of what transpired over the few days his parents were in Greenville was a mystery to Kevin. Apparently, Mom and Dad had convened with Art and Kathy in the office of the Park's pastor. Whether Sam was present, Kevin did not know. His parents spent time with Kevin as he was available between his other obligations. Kevin inferred that his dad had spoken with other pastors or counselors, but he did not know the extent of those conversations. The university was notified at some level.

For his part, Kevin had one session of "counseling" with his dorm supervisor. Matt was a great guy, a mentor of sorts and a friend. He was not qualified to help. His conversation with Kevin centered around the providence and goodness of God. He gave Kevin a copy of a book by Jerry Bridges titled Trusting God. He encouraged the distraught survivor to forgive Sam and to write him a letter of forgiveness. Kevin wrote the letter and dropped it in the mail.

There was a phone call with his future father-in-law and more time just getting off campus with Mom and Dad before they headed home.

A few days later, he stopped by his P.O. Box and found a note from Sam, a request for forgiveness. Kevin kept the note.

Kevin scouted the tiny condo and decided to accept the offer. He moved his few belongings from campus to the north side of Greenville. His parents eventually brought a few items from Glenford to help furnish the home. With a bathroom in the center, the layout was simple. You entered into a tiny living and dining room combined with a kitchenette. That was half of the unit. Two bedrooms were on the opposite side. With ease, the entire house would have fit into the basement back home in Glenford. Kevin was happy regardless. This would be his space. With no roommates, no guys sharing the bathroom and his bride soon to join him, he was content.

His job during that last semester at Bob Jones was at MCI World-Com. Along with other former and current students, he was a tele-marketer offering consumers discounted rates for long distance calls. Little did he know that he was at the end of an era. Not long after, the company would collapse. He did not love the work. Constant rejec-tion, even when you're getting paid, is a form of masochism enjoyed by few. But the few sales each night buoyed his spirits, and the job paid better than his previous on-campus responsibility. He could also escape campus and the frustration caused by his living arrangement.

Dorm rooms at Bob Jones were small. Each room had five beds, but generally, only two to three men were assigned to a room. The extra beds were sometimes filled by university guests. Kevin had never had more than two roommates during his first six semesters. He had even enjoyed one semester with just one roommate. Stephen was the guy's name, and he was as neat and tidy and quiet as Kevin Stephens.

Kevin anticipated something similar for his final semester. He was wrong. Trouble began the first night. The university required that he check-in no later than Sunday evening at 10:00 PM. Wanting to see his fiancée before getting to Greenville, Kevin left Ohio on Wednesday headed for Tennessee. Visiting Tiffany was fun, and he did not want to go on to BJU. Unusually for him, he waited until the last moment to leave. He was roughly six hours from school when he kissed her goodbye. A one-hour time change also had to be considered. With a heavy foot on the gas pedal, he raced across Tennessee on I-40 making good time. Too good. Flashing lights appeared in his rearview mirror, and his heart sank. He pulled his white Chevy Corsica to the side of the highway.

"Good afternoon, sir. License and registration. What has you speeding through Tennessee?" the officer asked having already observed the Ohio license plate.

"I just left my fiancée's, and I'm headed back to college."

"You were doing nearly ninety miles an hour. The speed limit is only seventy."

"I'm sorry, officer. The road was clear, and I'm in danger of being late."

"You're in danger of being dead."

Kevin rolled his eyes but only inwardly. "Write the dumb ticket," he thought, "And let me go."

"Wait here," the patrolman commanded as he collected Kevin's drivers license and car registration. He stalked back to his vehicle as Kevin fumed.

Minutes passed. At last, the officer returned.

"You're lucky I'm not giving you a ticket for speeding in a work zone."

"What?!" All of Kevin's self-control was required not to scream. Lucky? "Yes, sir, I was not in the work zone."

"You were a mile away. I could have added that to the ticket."

Oh, now Kevin was really struggling. *I'm lucky that you did not give me a ticket for a violation that I did not incur? Yeah, real lucky.*

"Thank you, sir," he managed, but he feared the tone of his voice did not mask his anger.

"Be safe. You have a few hours of driving ahead of you. Try to make it there alive."

Kevin had no response. He put his window up and slowly pulled away. Entering the work zone at an even fifty-five miles per hour, he continued to replay the words in his brain. That smacked of an abuse of authority to him. He knew he deserved the ticket. That was fine. But to be threatened and to be treated like this officer was doing him a favor by only writing a ticket for the actual infraction and not adding a bogus charge? Kevin was furious.

Carefully observing the speed limit for the rest of the trip, Kevin arrived on campus with minutes to spare. Then he received his room assignment. As he pieced together the data, he realized that he would spend his final semester in the most remote men's room on campus. He would be in the dorm furthest from everything. He would be in the furthest room of that dorm, and he would be on the topmost floor. He felt like he was being punished for not returning as a hall leader. *Oh well,* he thought, *I only have to survive one semester.*

His four-door sedan was stuffed with his dorm supplies. He pulled around to the dormitory and found a space as close to his end of the building as possible. Maybe he would only have one roommate. Maybe they buried another ex-hall leader up here with him. Trudging up the three floors to his hall, he had time to take many deep breaths. "Just one semester," he reminded himself.

When he opened the door to his room, his panic meter instantly shattered. Three guys were already in the room. Three. The best bunks and storage spaces were already taken. Three men were going to be in here with him for the entire semester. Not only that, but as they introduced themselves, he recognized the two upperclassmen. They were known troublemakers. The third guy was a pimple-covered freshman. Kevin was miserable.

So, because he had stepped aside from hall leading, they had stuck him in the worst room with the worst roommates. At least, that's how he felt. On top of that, he was expected to be the spiritual leader not only in this room but also to the men in the adjoining three rooms. Additionally, he no longer had any of the privileges of being a hall leader and would be accountable to the hall leader on the hall. That guy was wandering down the hallway now, introducing himself and making sure everyone was getting settled in.

"Stephens," he yelled.

Kevin turned. He did not know the guy by name but recognized his face.

"I'm Nathan. I don't know if you remember me."

"I don't think we've formally met," answered Kevin, "but I recognize your face. Brokenshire desk, right?"

Like Kevin, Nathan had worked at the checkout desk on the main floor of the men's dorm named for Brokenshire. None of the students knew who that person was, but they did know that to check-in and out of campus according to the rules, you had to communicate with the guys at the Brokenshire desk. Getting off campus was an ordeal. Students had to go to the office of the Dean of Students and meet with one of the Deans of Men or Women. They were only available for specific hours. You stood in line and then asked the dean for permission to leave campus. Without approval of your request, your departure would be unauthorized and leave you vulnerable to demerits or even expulsion.

Some permissions were granted for an entire semester. Others were only granted on a case-by-case basis. Once you had the dean's approval, you then had to show that permission slip to the checkout desk. Each night, the guys at the desk made sure everyone who had left during the day had checked back in by 10:25 PM. Any missing students were reported. Any students who returned but failed to check back in were given demerits.

In short, you could not leave campus without showing your face at the Brokenshire desk. For their part, the guys who worked shifts on the desk had to know the handbook well. And, in turn, they got to know most of the guys on campus since nearly everyone left at least occasionally. The Dean of Men considered the Brokenshire desk workers to be an extension of his office. Consequently, the guys who worked there were chosen with care. And because humans were involved, there was also a bit of politics.

Kevin was hired for the desk for his sophomore year, partly because he had a great personal reputation and mostly because his sister had served as part of the Dean of Women's office. Nathan had similar connections. Both had been promoted to hall leader, which was not automatic. Some of the Brokenshire guys did not become hall leaders. And conversely, guys were promoted to hall leader who had never served on the checkout crew.

Kevin had crossed paths with the younger classman the previous year. Nathan worked on the checkout crew while Kevin served as hall leader. Kevin would be the first to admit that he did not follow the check-in and check-out rules punctiliously. Some of his violations were accidental and some intentional. But he had followed the guidelines at times and had witnessed Nathan on occasion at the desk.

"I am so glad to have you on my hall," continued Nathan. "You're going to have to help me with these guys," and he gesture to Kevin's roommates. They laughed. Kevin did not.

"Hey, I'm still getting unpacked. I'll get with you later," Kevin informed Nathan. He jogged down the three flights of stairs and went back to his car. He got back in and considered his options. He had none. He was stuck. Quitting now would make no sense. His parents would not let him. Tiffany would be horrified, he imagined. Ugh. He got out and slammed the door. Popping the trunk open, he took another load to his room. He would not have time to fully unpack tonight. He made one more trip to pick up the essentials. Tomorrow, he would have time to finish settling into his cramped accommodations. Back at his room, he began covering the mattress on the top of the two-bed bunk. A bell rang. He had five minutes before prayer group. That was the evening routine at Bob Jones. You had to check-in and be on your hall by 10:25 PM. A five-minute warning bell would ring. At 10:30 PM, everyone was required to participate in a prayer meeting. For fifteen minutes, students gathered in the dorm room of their prayer captain (PC) and had a brief time of devotion and prayer. Kevin was expected to lead as the PC at his end of the hall. He laughed. This was ridiculous. Kevin valued authenticity. Spiritual issues were too important to just fake. He wanted to want to lead with sincerity. At this moment, however, he was sincerely pissed off. He finished the base sheet and sat in a chair. Three minutes until the men gathered in his room. Attempting to organize his thoughts, he buried his face in his broad hands.

"Hey, Kev," one of his rebel roommates interrupted, "keep the prayer group fun."

Kevin did not respond. He was in trouble.

He had survived that final, awful semester of college. He had moved into the tiny condo. He had endured the telemarketing job. Now, life was going to get better. He had resigned from MCI WorldCom. In fact, as he lay there in bed, he was getting paid vacation time by the company. His two weeks of vacation and his two-weeks' notice were put in simultaneously and approved by HR. He never had to go back to the cubicles and make another call. Instead, Kevin and Tiffany would be returning to move into the parsonage of Fellowship Baptist Church. For the past two years, they had attended Fellowship when they were in town, and they had participated in church life. Pastor Bryce Hager had asked Kevin to join the staff. Because Bryce had his own home, part of Kevin's compensation would be free board in the spacious brick ranch house on the church property. His commute would be exceedingly brief. While Tiffany was excited to start married life in the little condo, she did not mind the upgrade to a four-bedroom, two-and-a-half bath house. Some of the interior was aged and ugly, but Pastor Hager had given them permission to make any changes they wanted.

Kevin breathed deeply. A new job, a new home and a wife, life was going to be great.

He heard Barkley stirring and decided to get moving. Still in his black shorts and white tee from his night of rest, he checked in with his best friend.

"Want to get hitched?" asked Barkley.

"Well, this is an awkward proposal, and I'm already sworn to another, but let me think about it."

"That would make for a fun twist to the evening."

Their entire friendship was based on a mutual grasp of sarcasm, humor and good-natured ribbing.

"That may be cool in Canada, but I'm not sure Tennessee is ready." Kevin took a shot at Barkley's home country. A native of Manitoba, Barkley was used to being asked if he had a dog sled and if he lived in an igloo. Neither were applicable. On trips home for the holidays, he had offered to bring back Canadian specialties for Kevin.

"Bring me some Canadian M&Ms," Kevin would request. Barkley never did.

"Tennessee is not ready, and independent Baptists are not ready. Frankly, I'm not ready. You're not really my type, Stephens. Sure, we'd make each other laugh. But there's more to marriage, right?"

"I'll let you know," Kevin assured him.

"That's why I'm letting you get married first," said Barkley. "If you find out that it's terrible, let me know before July. I'll break Jen's heart Jen-tly," he punned.

Kevin laughed. "If it's miserable, I'm just going to let you suffer, too."

Their host interrupted them with an offering of breakfast which they gladly accepted. The day was already scheduled. In a short while, Kevin would swing by the bed and breakfast to check-in and make sure everything was set for that night. Then he and Barkley would pick up tuxes, head to the church and prepare for pictures around 3:00 PM. The ceremony would begin at 6:00 PM. By 7:30 PM, they would be at the reception. From there, Barkley would drive them the short distance to their honeymoon cabin. Kevin's dad would serve as best man. His sisters were already in town. Tiffany's father would officiate.

They expected around two hundred people, many of them from out-of-town. Church family from Milwaukee and Glenford were making the trip. And several were coming over from Greenville, too. Tiffany's father, Dan, was a notorious miser. If the only mark of a fool was that he and his money were soon parted, Dan would go to his grave as one of the wisest.

Tiffany was paying for the bulk of the wedding from money she had saved while employed as a bank teller. To save money, she had used as many of her father's tricks as she could while still buying a beautiful new dress and having fresh flowers. Much of the food was provided by a family in her church that owned an Asian restaurant. Kevin had voiced his opinion when asked but work and school had occupied his mind. The most time he had spent with Tiffany since the end of the summer was over new year's. They spent Y2K together in case the computers destroyed the world. Fortunately, the world survived.

Life was changing for his parents, too. Mom and Dad had resigned from the church in Glenford and moved to Milwaukee. Dad would serve on the staff at the church Dan Johnson had started twenty-four years earlier. The web of connections was thick. With the marriage of Kevin and Tiffany the degrees of separation were shrinking. Everyone seemed to agree that this union was inevitable and providential. What could be better than this close alignment of influential families?

The afternoon and evening passed smoothly. Pictures were taken by the hundreds. Tiffany looked beautiful in her lace gown. Fresh lilies and violet roses sprinkled the pew ends, the bouquets and the boutonnieres.

Friends and family gathered in the auditorium. Every seat was filled, and some were standing in the rear.

Kevin took his place on the platform with his father, Barkley and his young brother-in-law, Jon. Kevin often joked that he would be the best man at his wedding. As he explained to his family, "I think it's rude for the bride to show up and not get the best man." Still, he bestowed on his father the role.

As he stood on the platform, he thought he was prepared for this moment. Then the music started for the processional. When Tiffany stepped through the doors accompanied by Dan, his emotions were too powerful. Tears poured down his cheeks. He had a handkerchief in his pocket that he did not expect to use. Within minutes, the thin material was soaked.

Dan and Dad both spoke. Music was performed. Kevin focused on Tiffany's face. He was able to choke back his feelings just enough to enunciate his vows. Tiffany also said, "I do." They kissed, a tasteful Baptist smooch on the lips. Down the aisle they walked, arm-in-arm, married at last.

More than a reception, the lively gathering at a nearby hall felt like a reunion. Kevin and Tiffany made a round of greetings, cut the cake, grabbed the cards and made an exit within about an hour's time. Barkley chauffeured them to the bed and breakfast cabin just a few minutes further from the party.

They entered the beautiful, rustic accommodations and collapsed on a love seat, kissing and conversing, re-living the highlights of the evening.

"I didn't expect you to be so emotional," the bride observed. "Mom said you started crying as soon as I entered the room."

"And not the last time that will happen," Kevin joked. "Yeah, I tried not to cry. I failed."

"It's okay. I thought I would cry more."

"Some of us aren't heartless," he smirked at her.

"Is it too soon to slap you?"

"Definitely. We need at least six months of the honeymoon phase before you get violent."

"I could never hit you," she assured him and gave him a kiss. "But I think a smack is different. I'm ready to get out of this dress." She stood. "I may need some help. Would you be a gentleman and help me?"

"Oh, I'll help." He jumped up. "But I won't be a gentleman."

Wedding dresses do not slip off easily. They are dissembled in stages. As he helped her with hooks and snaps and buttons and clasps, he slowly unveiled her body.

"I want to take a bath with you before we get in bed." Tiffany had read that this was a good first step towards mental and physical preparation.

"Then help me out of my clothes."

His came off much more easily. Soon, they stood before each other, fully naked for the first time. Tiffany looked at his full erection and gasped slightly.

"That goes inside of me?"

Kevin wasn't sure if he should be proud or concerned.

They started the water running in the giant tub. Tiffany added bubbles. They sat at opposite sides facing each other, their legs overlapping each other's. The hot water was relaxing. Darkness had already fallen before they entered the cabin. Time had slipped towards midnight when they toweled off and headed up to the king-sized bed in the loft.

They pulled back the covers and climbed onto the large, soft mattress. Tiffany lay down on her back. Kevin hovered over her. He did not detect a lot of interest.

"Do you want to sleep first? We can make love in the morning," he offered.

"No, I want to feel you. Go ahead."

This was not quite the passion he had envisioned. He tried suggestions from the books he had read. Giving her full body his attention, he moved to her vagina at last and patiently used his tongue and fingers to explore.

"Are you okay?" he inquired. "How does that feel?"

"It's okay. Keep going."

He spread his legs and slowly entered her. She was quiet.

"Does that feel good?"

"Um. It's different."

Again, not the words he expected.

"You can just finish," she said. "We can try again tomorrow."

Kevin was feeling some deep emotions. This was a much different experience than he hoped for. He felt strange inside. This was supposed to be mutual affection and desire. Still, her body felt good, and he climaxed quickly with her permission. He moved to her side and sought to give her the aftercare that he had gleaned from the textbooks. She was reluctant to cuddle.

"I need to clean up," she said. She went to the bathroom, and Kevin grabbed a bottle of water. When she was finished, he took his turn, giving her a quick kiss as she passed him. By the time he got back in bed, she was curled up under the covers already asleep.

He kissed her once again on the cheek and got comfortable with his pillow and coverings. As alone with his thoughts as he had ever been, he felt the stillness to his core. The loop of his rape was still playing in his head. He had anticipated that this fresh start with his new bride would erase the old horrors. Instead, he felt familiar pain, guilt and despair.

Again, he found himself praying, "Forgive me, God."

Chapter Nine

Day 7

His pregnant wife beside him, Kevin stood in the lobby of the Maranatha Bible Church. He was standing in a space that had previously been the church office of his childhood. The heavy steel desk where he had colored for hours and answered the phone was now downstairs. Two walls of the office had been removed to create more room for the parishioners who came early and stayed late after services.

"What do you think?" he asked Tiffany.

"I can't imagine they would say no. Everyone seems to think you'll be a great pastor."

Inside the auditorium, the church members were casting votes to select Kevin as their next pastor, only the third in their twenty-seven-year history. Mom and Dad had been in Milwaukee for nearly three years. Without them, the congregation struggled. Dad had helped them find a new pastor through the church in Wisconsin. Brent was different. His family was different. They had not been a good fit in Glenford.

Part of the issue was Dad's long shadow cast by years of building relationships. He had been kind and patient and yet had pushed for excellence. Any man would've been hard-pressed to fill those shoes.

For two years, Brent and the church searched for commonality and comfort. They could not find homeostasis. The Halstead family left. For nine months the core families of the church looked for another candidate. They argued. They invited men to fill the pulpit. They asked other churches for recommendations. They held business meetings and argued some more.

Early in the process, the church secretary had an idea. Their former pastor's son was an assistant pastor in Greenville, South Carolina. The church should consider him.

On a Sunday night in March, Kevin took a phone call from the secretary.

"Would you be open to serving as our pastor?"

Kevin responded with mixed emotions. Going home had always been a desire. He loved Glenford. He cared about the people. Maybe this was a good idea. Yet, he was not his father. While he shared some of the temperament, his convictions and personality were solely his own.

"I'll pray about it," he offered. "And if the pulpit committee asks me for my resume, I will send it for their consideration."

Nancy was thrilled. This was a good start.

Weeks passed. Kevin prepared his resume, but a request was not received. He saved the document to his hard drive and waited.

When Glenford called again, a pulpit committee member was on the other end.

"Hey, Kevin, it's Dale."

Dale had known Kevin since he was in diapers. Dale's wife, Mary, had changed a few of those diapers.

"We thought we had a pastor lined up, but the congregation voted no. We're back at square one. Would you mind sending us your resume? I can't promise that we'll consider you, but we'll add it to the stack and treat you like everyone else."

Kevin acquiesced. Weeks passed. He found out later that his resume had been put on the bottom of the stack. He would be the last resort. This did not offend him at all. He was twenty-four years old. While he had a lot of maturity, was an excellent speaker and knew church life well, he was still learning.

The third call from Glenford came from yet a different individual. Mark was a member of the pulpit committee. He was also the secretary's son-in-law.

"We're still working through the process here," he offered almost apologetically. "Other men are being considered."

"Makes sense to me," Kevin assured him.

"In the meantime, we'd like to do Vacation Bible School for the children this summer. Would you be interested in coming up and running that for us?"

"I'll need to confer with my pastor first, of course. If he's okay with me being gone, I would enjoy helping you."

Bryce was not surprised. "You have been a great help to us. You should go. Hopefully, we get to keep you here for a long time. But if something works out where you end up leaving, I know you're ready for the next step."

"I don't think it will get that far," Kevin protested. "I think it will honestly just be helping with Bible school. They'll find a pastor soon."

The church did not.

Tiffany was showing a baby bump now. Constantly asked if he was excited, Kevin preferred to take one day at a time. Marriage had not been easy. The first night of their honeymoon had set the stage for their home life. They were good friends. Rooming together was easy. But sexual life was not as romantic as Kevin had anticipated. Their attempts at lovemaking became fewer for a year. Then Tiffany decided she wanted a baby. She finally initiated sex. But Kevin felt used as she made her intentions clear. Yes, she wanted to have sex but not for him. He did not feel loved or wanted. His best attempts to woo her were met with verbal gratitude and physical indifference.

He reread the books. He read additional books. At last he consulted with his pastor.

"We're struggling," he confided in Bryce. "Tiffany doesn't enjoy sex."

Bryce empathized. "It's not uncommon. Keep working at it together. You'll figure it out. Every married couple has issues."

What Kevin left out was a truth that he was loathe to share. His wife's rejection was prompting negative feelings resulting from his experience of sexual trauma. Humiliated enough by the admission of bedroom troubles, Kevin was not willing to add any further hurt to the equation.

When Tiffany finally got a positive result of pregnancy, she was thrilled. Some of her concern had revolved around family issues of infertility. She was not incapable of bringing life into the world. She was normal. Sex dissipated again. Every time she offered her body without enthusiasm, Kevin felt like a rapist. He initiated less and less, protecting himself from her rejections. She did not seem to mind.

Tiffany was excited to get out of Greenville. She was looking forward to helping with Bible school. Kevin and Tiffany prepared the materials and sent them ahead. Scheduled for the middle of July, Kevin asked for two weeks of vacation. Pastor Hager and the deacons approved.

After a few conversations with Mark, the itinerary had come together. The young couple would arrive on a Wednesday. Kevin would speak at the Bible study. Then he would lead an organizational meeting for the volunteers helping with VBS. He and Tiffany would make a quick trip to West Virginia to see Nanny and Papa on Thursday and

Friday. On Saturday, they would be back in Glenford for any final preparations. Kevin would preach in both services on Sunday.

The last time they had visited Glenford was two years prior. Invited to attend the 25th anniversary, Kevin took his young bride back, their first trip to Glenford as a married couple. Mom and Dad and his sisters had all participated. A lot of reminiscing occurred. While the church had changed, many core families from his childhood remained. Most of those people were still there, he discovered. That Wednesday night passed quickly. The private conversations were few. Complaints about the previous pastor were shared. Kevin avoided those conversations with tact and grace.

"I'm sure he meant well. That was a tough position for him to be in. How can I help you right now?"

Most of the help was listening, sympathizing and offering hope for the future.

Kevin was glad they were limiting their time for now. The quick check-in and escape to Nanny's and Papa's was well-planned. Kevin's sense of justice made him uncomfortable focusing on the former pastor as the sole source of conflict. He heard nothing that indicated the man was nefarious. At worst, he was oblivious and clumsy. People need help adjusting to change. The process is helped by patience and wisdom. Brent made errors in communication and timing. Had the congregation been patient, he would likely have improved. This was his first-time pastoring, after all.

The only change in the venture to Clarksburg in the intervening years was the increased speed limit on Route 50. Nanny and Papa were happy to have company. Tiffany had never been to Kevin's grandparent's home. She had heard all about Nan's chocolate pie. One was waiting on the counter when they walked in.

Kevin hugged his grandmother and said, "Nan, I am going to intentionally make a relationship mistake."

She waited with an intrigued grin.

"I've never compared Tiffany's cooking to my mother's or anyone else's. I have not criticized her efforts in the kitchen, and I have not complained. But today, I am going to beg you to teach her your recipe."

Tiffany and Nan laughed. Tiffany had tried to make chocolate pie for Kevin before they were married. In the process, the pudding became lumpy. Hastily, she grabbed a colander looking for a way to remove the lumps. She threw the colander in the sink and dumped the pudding. Her one mistake was not placing a pot on the underside to catch the pudding that oozed through. In her frustration and disgust, she washed it all down the sink and gave up. She made other chocolate desserts, but chocolate cream pie was not on the menu.

Two days elapsed like two hours. Back to Glenford they headed. On Sunday, Kevin preached. His speaking had evolved since his early efforts as a teenager. Those who had heard him speak even during his tenure as an intern noticed the change. Blending insight with humor, he took his listeners deep into the biblical text before making practical applications. Forty minutes later, many would have sat and listened for another forty, or so they said. Feedback was overwhelmingly positive. The afternoon was the exact scenario Kevin had foreseen and mostly circumvented on Wednesday. People wanted to talk about the issues with Brent and the difficulty with finding another pastor. After the service, over lunch, before the evening service and afterwards, the people changed, but the conversations were roughly the same.

Kevin felt like a broken record. "I'm sorry. That's tough. You have every right to feel frustrated. What do you think God is doing in all of this?"

Kevin was struggling with his own, "What do you think God is doing?" Back in the building where he was raped as a kid, the feelings were deep, profound and unsettling. The old bathroom was unchanged with the exception of a broken tile. Kevin shoved his feelings aside. He had tried to get help. There were no answers. Forgive and forget. Trust God. Move on.

Here, no one knew about the childhood rapes except Tiffany. She had no similar experience. He couldn't share his pain with her. She did not understand.

Plenty of volunteers were prepared to help. Kevin would focus on the teens and adults. Others would teach the children. Every night during VBS, he led the music. He had written the theme song for the week, which he taught them. The other songs were familiar at least to the church kids. Kevin was increasingly concerned about connecting with individuals who did not regularly attend church. He wanted to help the people who were hurting like he was, who felt distant from God and unseen by believers. They were the ones who truly needed compassion.

In the middle of the week, Kevin was approached by the church leaders.

"Would you be able to stay and preach all day on Sunday?" they requested.

"Yes." His two weeks of vacation left that weekend open.

VBS was considered a resounding success. Largely the work of the volunteers, Kevin made sure to express his gratitude. While he and Tiffany served in the spotlight, many others labored in the shadows to accomplish the real work of the ministry.

This was a perspective that Kevin had grown to appreciate as an assistant. Servant leadership was a concept that he had been introduced to as a counselor and a hall leader. Several sermons echoed that truth, too. Kevin believed his responsibility as an assistant pastor was to make Bryce look good. Much of his work was overshadowed by Pastor Hager. Kevin did not mind. Praise made him uncomfortable.

Another weekend of speaking and listening, speaking and listening. Years later, Kevin would reflect on the irony of pastoral work. Everyone thought that you got to speak all the time. Most of ministry was not speaking. His most meaningful work was listening. Although he was granted the opportunity to speak publicly without interruption for one hundred and twenty minutes or so per week, he would spend hours every day listening to God and parishioners.

Nanny would often chide, "You have two ears and one mouth. Listen twice as much as you speak." Those were wise words but also peculiar coming from a lady who would gab on the phone with neighbors every night for hours.

The second Sunday passed, and the pulpit committee asked for another meeting.

"We think you might be the right pastor for the congregation. Would you be willing to pray about it and come back in August to candidate officially?"

Kevin was overwhelmed, humbled. He was also not surprised. He, too, had sensed that he was ready. Tiffany felt the same.

"I am going to agree tentatively, but I need to confirm that this is okay with Pastor Hager."

"Of course."

Pastor Hager was on board. "You're ready." He was a blunt man and not overly sentimental. "I've already talked to some of the men here. They agree. We'll pray about it with you, but you have our blessing."

Kevin clasped Tiffany's hand and stared at the floor. A mere twelve feet from where he was raped as a kid, he was now a man on the brink of the greatest responsibility of his young life.

He prayed. "God, you know that I cannot figure this out if it's anything less than obvious. Please make your will plain."

When the heavy door to the auditorium swung open into the foyer, Kevin had his answer. Mark was grinning. "Come on in, Pastor Stephens."

The pulpit committee was relieved. Fifty-two members attended the meeting. All of them voted in favor. That evening was a blur of congratulations and speculations about the transition. This was only the beginning. Much work needed to be done.

Evening receded into twilight. Outside the brick building, a handful of members talked as the moon rose and the stars twinkled. At last, Kevin and Tiffany got back to their room and into bed. With pregnancy wearing her out, she fell asleep quickly. Kevin did not. He lay in bed feeling the butterflies in his stomach. He was not nervous about the job ahead or the move or the prospect of adding a baby to the mix. What troubled him now was living in the shadow of his rapes. Compartmentalization had gotten him this far. But life had been easier in a different place. Now he would be home stepping into that space almost daily.

He wanted comfort. He wanted to be held. But he would not bother his pregnant wife. He rolled to his side and curled up as he once had on the basement landing. From the corner of his eye, a tear rolled down and dampened his pillow. He was coming home.

Chapter Ten

Day 8

Drenched in sweat, Kevin slowed the treadmill to a two-mile per hour crawl and allowed himself the luxury of a stroll. His workouts were exhausting, but they had transformed his body from the pudgy bulk of post-marital weight gain to a tight, muscular hulk. For a pastor, he was in amazing shape. Actually, for a human being he was in great shape. Daily habits had been shaped over years. Tiffany had been partly responsible for the discipline.

"You're fat," she told him bluntly about four years into their marriage.

He was stunned. She had gone through her own body changes through the course of marriage and pregnancy. He had never been anything but supportive, constantly affirming her beauty. This was a tidbit of wisdom he had gained from all the marriage materials he had absorbed.

Some time passed, but eventually, on a random April morning, he got up, strapped on tennis shoes and walked around the country block. Slightly less than a mile, he finished in about fifteen minutes. His knee was sore the next day, nevertheless he completed another lap. And the day after, his knee aching like a tooth gone bad, he completed another. On his fifth day, the knee pain subsided, and Kevin picked up the pace. By the end of the summer, he was running four miles per day, five days a week. From 230 pounds, he trimmed down to 180. Parishioners noticed. Some were concerned about his health.

"Do you have cancer?"

One of the men he counseled had a home gym and introduced him to lifting, particularly the bench press. Kevin began regaining weight, this time stacking muscle onto his frame. By the time he turned 27, he was a different man. And over the following years, while he varied the workouts, he kept himself fit.

As the treadmill ground on, Kevin began mentally ticking through his checklist of responsibilities for the day. Being a pastor was a full life. And he was now a father of three boys. Balance was not a word that he found helpful. Rather, life was about making daily priorities. Some days were mostly ministry. And others were mostly family. And as much as he could, he combined both. Today was going to be primarily ministry.

Wednesdays were capstoned by the midweek prayer service. Tonight, he would lead about 40 adults in a short but deep dive into a few verses of the Book of Proverbs. His Bible study was mostly prepared. Between now and then, he had a full day planned.

Kevin was an organized leader. Daily tasks were delineated from weekly and monthly responsibilities. But many days were interrupted with unexpected calls from people in the congregation, trips to the hospital for emergencies or the need for crisis counseling. Nine years of stressful ministry had matured him into a solid pastor. His sermons were deep and meaningful. His counsel was wise beyond his years. His influence was broad beyond his congregation. That impact had brought people into his congregation from an hour radius outside of Glenford. For a while the congregation had grown significantly.

On Sunday mornings the pews were full, and the atmosphere was often electric. Then there was some turmoil. Kevin had led a series of sermons toward a view of Christian living that was simple and beautiful. And in the process, he had slowly but surely trampled some sacred cows that were worshipped by traditionalists. His leadership was humble and compassionate, but he was also persistent. Then he partnered with a young evangelist to bring all of these truths into practical application. And the wheels came off. Several long-time members left. Kevin was crushed. Lots of hard conversations were held. Kevin was excoriated by some, appreciated by others. He really did not care. He thought he was doing the right thing, the best thing for his church family.

Kevin lost vision of where to go next, unsure of how to move the church forward.

Then he met Jeff. A Columbus fireman and brother-in-law to a longtime deacon at Maranatha, Jeff came to him with an unusual request.

They met for lunch at McDonalds in Buckeye Lake.

Kevin arrived first. He was always early. He was a Stephens. He watched as a small, beige sedan pulled into the parking lot and swung into a space. Jeff exited the vehicle and perambulated towards the door. He was shorter than Kevin's six-foot frame by about seven inches. His dark hairline was deeply receded. His face was cleanly shaven. He was neither thin nor fat. Firefighting had kept him in decent shape, although the fireman's love for food showed a bit at his waist. His eyes were dark but active and lively. He smiled often and had a quick sense of humor.

Bright sunlight could not prevent the bite of a cool, spring breeze, and Jeff wore a canvas jacket over a hunter green t-shirt. His Levis were a bit too long, bunching at his black boots.

He stepped through the doors and smiled broadly.

"Hi, Pastor! Thanks for meeting with me." He shook Kevin's hand with a solid grip. During his days off from the fire department, he laid tile. In fact, he had installed tiles in the foyer and bathrooms at Maranatha as part of a significant remodeling project. Jeff had ripped out the old mustard-based, swirly-colored cheap tile that haunted Kevin's childhood memories. In its place, he laid a beautiful, emerald ceramic tile. Kevin had welcomed the change even though the haunting nightmares continued.

"My pleasure, Jeff! I admire your craftmanship every day when I enter the church. That tile made a nice difference."

Jeff blushed. "Glad you approve. I appreciated the extra work. And thank you for supporting us through Jenna's illness."

Jeff's youngest daughter, Jenna, was a recent survivor of leukemia. Kevin had made a couple of trips to the children's hospital to offer support for the family, and the people of Maranatha had been supportive in various ways.

"I wish we could have done more, Jeff. I am happy to hear she's doing well. What sounds good for lunch? I'm buying."

Jeff attempted to decline. "I was planning to buy your lunch!"

Kevin laughed, "I'll let you pick up the tab when we eat at a more expensive restaurant."

Jeff smirked. "Oh, I get it now."

They ordered their burgers, fries and Cokes, picked up their food and found a table. Small talk ensued through lunch. Jeff finished his last fry, tidied up his tray and shifted uncomfortably.

"The reason I wanted to meet with you today is that we have some new bad news." He paused.

Kevin's heart sank. This was his life, holding space for wonderful people in terrible times.

"Several months ago, I noticed some numbness in my hands and feet. My doctor ran tests and nothing came back positive. And now he's pretty sure I have ALS. We don't know how quickly the disease will progress, but we do know that it definitely will."

Silence filled the space between them as Kevin absorbed the words. Both men's eyes filled with tears.

"Jeff. I am so sorry. That's heavy."

"Yeah. I wanted to talk to you because I need help getting through this journey, basically knowing I am going to die," Jeff paused. He was controlling his emotions well given the news. "I really appreciate the way you teach the Bible and the way you minister to families. I know this is a strange request, but," he paused and choked back emotion searching for words, "Will you help me die? Will you be there for my family?"

Kevin was overwhelmed. He struggled to hold back his own emotions. Ministry was often painful, but this was excruciating. Kevin thought of Jeff's wife and three daughters. He considered the uncertainty of the request. He knew enough of the disease to know that the commitment could be years.

"So, Jeff, it's somewhat easy for me to sit here and say yes, of course. I'm honored to be your friend and to help you in any way I can. I certainly want to support your family. I don't feel adequate, but I am going to believe that God brought us together for this purpose. And I will pray for your family and with your family and do what I can with God's help. Can we pray right now?"

Huddled over the small table in the busy restaurant, the two men prayed oblivious to the other patrons. Tears streamed down their cheeks and puddled on the table. Kevin finished his prayer and turned to an old coping mechanism that had helped him through hundreds of crises.

"Jeff, I don't know why we're upset. We have no idea what's going to happen. You could outlive me! Maybe you need to help me get through the valley of the shadow of death."

The reality struck them both, and they shared a chuckle.

"Life is strange like that," Jeff agreed.

"Yeah. We just don't know what we don't know. But based on what we do know, let's get together at least once a week and figure it out along the way." Kevin searched Jeff's face for approval.

Jeff's eyes lit up noticeably. "Yes. That's great. Thank you."

That was three years ago.

Jeff was no longer meeting with Kevin under his own power. The decline after the conversation at McDonalds had been slow but steady. At first, the two men continued to meet out at whatever spot of choosing they desired. A year later, Jeff had to give up driving. Kevin would pick him up and take him to eat. Occasionally, Kevin would drive Jeff to Columbus to the fire station to chat with his old team. A few times, Kevin took Jeff to his mom's house in Westerville. But the weekly meetings kept going. Now, Jeff was struggling to walk, and the visits were at his house. Jeff's body was breaking down steadily.

Kevin stepped off the treadmill and headed to the shower. He would clean up and pick up his youngest from kindergarten and drive him home. Then he would stop by the office to wrap up preparations for the evening service. And then he would head to Jeff's for a few hours so that Jeff's wife could go shopping.

The plan went according to expectations, and Kevin headed to Jeff's around 1:30 in the afternoon. He picked up some flowers for Jeff's wife along the way. Kevin's maxim was that the key to a happy life was continuous small treats, not just for himself but for others, too. He reached Jeff's home several minutes before he was scheduled to be there.

He knocked at the back sliding door and quickly stepped through into the kitchen without waiting for permission. He was family at this point. Gina was there, grabbing her purse.

"Hi, Pastor! Thank you for sitting with Jeff. He's been looking forward to seeing you. I'll be back in a bit."

"Take your time. No rush. And here's some flowers for Jeff." He winked at her.

She smiled. "He will love them." She grabbed a vase and filled the base with water and set the flowers temporarily.

"If you need anything, call me," she urged him. "If I need to, I can come right back."

"We will be fine," Kevin assured her. "Enjoy the afternoon."

Gina left, and Kevin headed towards the living room. Jeff was sitting in a deep-brown recliner.

"Hey!" Jeff snapped out of a doze, and his face lit up. "It's about time you got here."

Kevin chuckled. "I didn't want to interrupt your nap." Kevin reached out and grabbed Jeff's hand. Jeff's grip was gone. His hand felt broken and small. Kevin looked Jeff in the eyes and smiled before sitting in a matching recliner. Inside, he felt the deep sadness of knowing that his friend was fading.

"What are you watching today?" Kevin gestured towards the television. The History channel was on, but the volume was low.

"Oh, it's about World War 2," said Jeff. "I've been watching a lot of documentaries. Ask me anything."

"What was the Churchillian doctrine?"

"Okay, never mind."

They laughed.

For an hour they rambled through topics: World War 2, Ohio State football, national politics. Then Kevin turned the conversation.

"How are you doing spiritually, Jeff?"

Jeff smiled. "God is good. I would never have asked for this, but He is taking care of us."

Kevin's face was neutral. He understood the sentiment, but his own experience of God had been different. "Good, Jeff. Hey, I brought the elements for communion. Would you like to observe the Lord's Supper together?"

Jeff was ecstatic. "I am so glad you remembered! Yes. I haven't observed for a while.

Kevin retrieved the juice and wafers from his vehicle.

He knelt by Jeff's chair and shared a moment of prayer and scripture before they drank the small cup and ate the bread. Jeff wept. The simple ceremony meant something to him at that time that he could not express. Kevin felt the depth of Jeff's emotion while holding his own in check. All of his powers of compartmentalization were at work to keep from plunging into his own emotions. Little did he know how those abilities were about to be tested.

Sitting back in the other recliner, the conversation continued with talk of Jeff's girls and his mother. But as time passed, Jeff began to shift uncomfortably.

"What time is it, Pastor?"

"Almost 3:30."

Jeff's eyes shifted to the back door. "I was hoping Gina would be back by now."

"Oops. I told her to take her time." Kevin smiled. But Jeff did not smile back.

"Um, this is embarrassing, Pastor, but I really need to go to the bathroom. I hate to ask you this, but can you help me?"

Kevin's nerves fired on all cylinders. He fought back every emotion he was feeling and said, "Sure, Jeff. Let's go."

He lifted Jeff to his feet from the recess of the soft easy chair. Jeff shuffled along, but Kevin was the sole reason he was standing. Across the room they cautiously inched to the bathroom. Kevin pushed the door open, and they entered the small guest half bath that adjoined the great room.

"You're going to have to help me with my pants, too," Jeff admitted.

That's exactly what Kevin feared. But he understood. His poor friend no longer had the strength for even the most personal of needs.

Kevin paused with Jeff standing in front of the toilet and carefully pulled down his sweats and underwear. Lowering Jeff to the seat, he made sure he could steady himself and left the room. He might as well have stayed. The damage was done. Jeff was humiliated. Kevin was triggered even though that definition of the word was not yet in his comprehension. Thankfully, Jeff only had to urinate and was quickly done. Kevin reentered and helped him stand. Then he pulled up Jeff's underwear and sweatpants. He helped him wash his hands, and then they took the journey back across the living room to the recliner. When Kevin lowered Jeff into the chair, he could feel the relief in Jeff's body and mind. The worst was over for his friend. He had survived the embarrassment of depending on his pastor to use the restroom. For Kevin, relief would not come for a long time. This was another cut, another bruise on an already deeply wounded psyche. He had no tools for processing the feelings attempting to hijack his nervous system. He could only quell them through sheer willpower.

The awkwardness between them passed, and they resumed their conversation for another half hour. When Gina entered, she caught them by surprise.

"I'm home just in time to make dinner," she announced.

"And just in time for me to head home for mine," Kevin replied. He said his goodbyes and stepped out the sliding glass door onto the deck and across the driveway to his minivan. As he went through the motions of starting the vehicle, buckling up and pulling away, he finally let the emotions escape. Tears of sadness trickled down his cheeks, touched the corners of his lips and cascaded off his chin. By the time he traveled the thirty minutes home, he had steeled himself. Parking in his driveway, he entered his own home to the cacophony of three boys eight years old and younger.

"Daddy's home! Daddy's home!" They piled into his arms. He hugged them, teased them and wrestled them to the ground. His wife never left the kitchen to greet him. She simply called out, "Dinner will be ready soon."

The four human beings who shared his space could not know the weight on his soul. He gave them the attention he could, but his focus was distracted. On the outside, he looked hale and vibrant. He entertained his family through dinner, readied himself for the evening Bible study and executed at a high level. No one suspected anything was amiss, not even the woman who shared his bed. And bed was where the mind unleashed its secrets. In his sleep, he re-lived the trauma of his youth.

The long day finally over, he sat in his underwear on the edge of the bed. His wife read a book. He wanted to tell her, but he couldn't. She would not understand. But he needed release.

"I had an awkward moment with Jeff today," he finally blurted out.

Laying on her side, her pillow propping up her head, she did not look up from her book.

"Yeah? What was awkward?"

"Jeff needed to use the restroom while Gina was gone. I had to take him."

"That is awkward," she agreed, then added, "Probably more for him than you."

"He was embarrassed for sure. Poor guy. This disease sucks."

"Well, good for you, being willing to help him. You've already been feeding him, might as well add bathroom duties to your friendship."

"I can't."

"People do it all the time, Kevin. Nurses do it. Kids help their parents. It happens."

"I know, but I am not a nurse. And it would be uncomfortable if it was my dad, too. I can't."

She finally lifted her eyes from the book, rolled towards him and asked, "What do you mean you can't?"

He didn't want to explain. Regret filled him. This was a conversation he now wished he had never started. "It reminds me of what Sam did to me."

"How?"

"I don't know. It just does."

"I'm sorry. That doesn't totally make sense to me, but I believe you. So, don't do it again." She rolled back over, found the paragraph where she left off and resumed her reading.

That was the kind of advice he had been receiving his whole life: Just don't. If he could just not, he would. He could not just turn off the pain, the hurt, the confusion, the guilt, the anxiety. He turned out his light and laid down. Pulling the comforter to his chin, he stared at the ceiling and tried to think of something else, anything else. He rolled towards Tiffany and put his arm around her.

"Good night," she whispered. And that was that. He rolled away from her and curled into the fetal position that had given him comfort many times. Tomorrow was Thursday, and he had work to do.

Chapter Eleven

Day 9

November was generally Kevin's favorite month. Trees were shedding the last vestiges of autumn. Harvests were mostly complete. Temperatures in Ohio were comfortable during the day and a bit chilly in the evening. He could go back to his favorite article of clothing, the quarter zip sweater. Low maintenance and comfortable, the sweaters were the fulcrum of his style. He could pivot to a casual look with jeans and t-shirt, or he could present a bit dressier with slacks and a collared shirt. He could even add a tie and show up for church.

But as he rolled out of bed and stumbled toward the shower on this Tuesday morning, he knew that today he would rock a gray quarter zip with a blue oxford shirt and a pair of black slacks. He had no time for a workout today. Instead, this would be a marathon morning of prepping the kids for school, dropping them off, and heading to Columbus for a conference.

As he entered the bathroom, he glanced back at the bundle of covers hiding his wife. Tiffany would be staying home. Shutting the door quietly, he waited until the latch set in place before flicking on the lights. His ritual was to stand completely nude on the scale before starting the hot water for his shower. Slipping out of his boxer briefs, he sat to piss so that his weight would not be inflated by the waste. Every ounce mattered. He didn't know why. His body looked great. His workouts were as consistent as ever, and his diet was fairly clean. Pausing in front of the mirror before he stepped on the scale, he saw the sculpted shoulders and solid chest of a man capable of bench pressing over three hundred pounds. His eyes went to his belly, lean but not chiseled. His enjoyment of chocolate was his Achilles heel. Still, he looked fit and trim. He stood on the scale and watched the digital numbers rapidly formulate a number – 208. On his six-foot frame, the pounds were mostly muscle. He breathed deeply. Right now, 210 was the Rubicon he would not cross. He had been weighing in between 205 and 210 for months.

Back across the small, tiled floor he paced to the tub, reached in and set the shower to one degree shy of molten lava. He stepped into the steaming stream from the opposite side and allowed himself to relax. Shower time was thinking time, planning time, dreaming time. He gave himself plenty of space for this act of self-care before he awakened the boys and started the process of dressing children and making breakfast. Rising at 5:30 AM to give himself an hour to contemplate was worth the loss of sleep. In the shower, he roused himself without caffeine. Coffee was not his daily habit. Tiffany needed the dark liquid. He did not. A certain pride filled his chest to be independent of the habit. Really, he could not drink the stuff without adding hundreds of calories to create a flavor he enjoyed. He preferred to save his junk calories for chocolate.

As he acclimated to the scalding water, he rolled his neck and flexed from head to toe. Then he took deep breaths and attempted to relax himself. He wasn't just attending a conference in Columbus. Another plan was also in the works.

Six months earlier, a chance encounter had changed his life. He had a gym membership at a fitness center in a strip mall anchored by Giant Eagle, a large grocery store. The long string of shops included a jeweler, sundry bakeries, restaurants, massage shops and a hair salon. His hair was low maintenance. He kept the length slightly longer than a black ant standing straight up. He often shaved his own head over the bathtub. But he appreciated a good, clean neckline, and for that, he needed a stylist. Plus, he didn't mind not having to clean up the mess. So occasionally, he would stop by the salon for a quick trim after leaving the gym.

"Easiest customer you'll have all day," he would assure the stylist. He preferred a woman to cut his hair, a preference shaped by his childhood trauma. He had gotten to know a few women over the years. In fact, his stylist that day was a lady who had cut his hair before, Trixie. She smiled at him as he walked through the door.

"I'll be with you shortly. I am almost done," she informed him while making final snips to the hair of the old gentleman seated in the chair.

"No rush," Kevin replied. He signed in and took a seat in one of the sterile, plastic chairs lined against the front window. Pulling out his phone, he opened his Bible app and continued thinking about his Sunday sermon. Kevin was a thinker, a processor. Sermons were not just concocted in the study. The ingredients were assembled in the study, but they simmered in his heart and mind all week long. By Saturday, he was ready to put the finishing touches on the Sunday meal. He usually came to the morning service with a four-course dinner of biblical exegesis, insight, illustration and application.

Deep in thought, Trixie had to get his attention, "Kevin! I'm ready for you now."

He looked up and discovered the previous customer was gone. He and Trixie were alone.

"Sorry about that. Let's go! Easiest money you'll make all day."

She laughed. "Yeah, I remember you. We're going to run clippers over your whole head with a number two guard, right? Clean up the neckline and make sure to clean off all the loose hair?"

"You know me well," Kevin laughed.

"Well enough," Trixie replied, and she got to work.

Kevin closed his eyes and relaxed as she wrapped the apron around his neck and then tucked in the paper to protect his clothes from the small clips of hair that were about to fly. Trixie picked up the clippers and turned them on. The hum became louder as she neared his scalp and began to comb through his hair. Little clumps of dark hair began to fall in his lap.

Above the buzz of the hairdresser's tool, he heard another sound, the clack of heels on the linoleum tile. And he heard a voice.

"Hey, Trixie! I washed the towels and stacked them. Do you need a fresh one?" Loud but not obnoxious, clear and bright, the voice caught Kevin's ear like music. He opened his eyes. What he saw surpassed all expectations. His eyes caught her black heels and followed up her long legs to her knee-length pencil skirt, black and simple but beautiful. Her cream camisole was covered with a thin black sweater, a protection against the constant air conditioning. Her face was thin with full pink lips amplified by lipstick. Her blue eyes stood out against the dark outline of mascara and eyeliner. Her thin black eyebrows capped a soft, beautiful expression of curiosity and poise. She was beyond beautiful. He looked her in the eyes, and she returned his gaze, neither boldly nor shyly. She smiled at him.

"Well, you must be new here. How have I never crossed paths with you before?"

"I'm usually here in the morning, and my haircuts last about as long as ice cream in summer."

Her eyes were bright. "Not a bad analogy. But I think we can do better." She laughed. "Watch out for this one, Trixie. He's not your average man from Licking County."

She winked at him. "I'm Holly, by the way, since Trixie is too busy to introduce us."

"I'm Kevin." He had met thousands of strangers, many of them attractive women. He was used to being a gentleman and making eye contact, showing respect and moving to the next person. Holly was different. He was captivated. How had he never seen her before?

Trixie paused, "I'm almost done. You're right, Holly. He's not your average Licking County man. He smells too good. Let's get these loose hairs off." Trixie commenced to brush him off with a towel. Holly made eye contact again.

"Make sure you come back around the same time. I enjoy a man who communicates with analogies. Throw in a simile or a metaphor, and I might marry you."

Kevin could not say much. He didn't want to interfere with Trixie fussing over him, and he really was at a loss for words.

"For sure," he responded. And he flashed a mischievous smile. She saw. And she walked away.

Two weeks later, he returned. He had not done much to his hair in the meantime other than to shave his neck. When he entered, Holly was busy with a client, a grandmotherly type. He wasn't sure he would get the same reaction with other people in the room. Little did he know.

"Ladies and gentlemen," Holly announced, "Here's a man who knows how to articulate." She turned to her client. "Let me tell you, Judy, this might be the most intelligent man in Heath."

He felt himself blush.

"Trixie isn't here, so you better sign up to let me do your haircut," Holly continued.

"Yes, ma'am," he managed, feeling anything but articulate or intelligent. His brain was mush.

Holly continued to talk to Judy and to include Kevin in the conversation. "Judy, when was the last time you met a man who could communicate?"

Judy thought. "Well, the salesman who got me to buy my vacuum was a pretty slick talker."

"Oh, I don't think this one is slick, Judy. Look at that face. He is as honest as they come."

Judy looked. "He does have an honest face."

Kevin was both mortified and entertained. "People do seem to trust me easily."

"What do you do for a living?"

"Promise you won't judge me?"

"Of course, I won't judge you...unless you're a vacuum salesman." Holly and Judy laughed. Kevin noticed smirks and grins from other clients who were enjoying Holly's sass.

"I'm a pastor."

"Shut. Up." Her face was radiant. She smiled at him. "You're a pastor? I guess that explains why you talk so well."

"I try," he shrugged.

"Okay, pastor. Let me get Judy out of these foils, and I'll get to you shortly."

Holly and Judy made their way to the back of the salon. As if the sun had passed behind a cloud, the front of the room became quiet and gray. Other stylists murmured to their clients and one another. Guests came and went. Kevin waited.

What felt like eternity was about fifteen minutes. The sun returned.

"Doesn't Judy look amazing?" Holly asked, seemingly speaking to no one and everyone. She was staring directly at Kevin.

"You are a fantastic stylist. She looks fabulous."

"Thank you. I don't want to take all the credit. Tell him, Judy. Tell him how you take care of those gorgeous locks of hair."

Judy laughed. "I use egg in my hair once a week. I have been doing that for the last thirty-seven years."

"Guess who needs some eggs, Kevin? You do. Better start now."

She rang Judy out. "You're the best, Judy! I will see you in a few weeks."

Judy walked out of the salon beaming.

"Your turn, cowboy. Get in my chair."

Kevin walked to the chair and sat down. Her complete attention was now on him. They knew nothing and everything about each other. He was drawn to her charismatic beauty, and she was attracted to his deep soul. He was facing the mirror as she stepped behind him. She paused. They looked into the mirror together briefly, catching a glimpse of togetherness. Enormous smiles swept their faces.

"Okay, mister. What are we doing here?"

"Well, you're the professional. Make me look good."

"You look great already, but this hair is not doing you any favors. I'll see what I can do, but you need to let it grow out a little longer up top over the next couple of weeks before you see me again."

The confidence caught him off-guard. Again? She wanted to see him again.

As if she could read his thoughts, she continued, "Oh, I am cutting your hair for the foreseeable future, Kevin. You're getting my business card, and you need to set your appointments directly with me. Otherwise, we're never going to get you styling."

He had never experienced attention from a woman like this. Part of him believed she was just a great salesperson and professional, but he also wondered if some other intention lingered behind the persona. He liked her immediately, immensely. She reminded him of his Nan, mischievous and sassy. Her way with people was easy and fun.

As she put her clippers together and began to run the vibrating scissors through his hair, she touched him with familiarity, as if she had been his barber for years. Her nails were polished and manicured. Everything about her was feminine and charming and...he searched for the word, joyful. She was free-spirited, and he envied and admired her all at once.

Kevin relaxed and let her work. She chattered a bit about other clients. Then she began to ask him questions.

"How long have you been a pastor?"

"I've been in Glenford for almost ten years. And I pastored in South Carolina for a couple of years."

"You look too young for that."

"I get that a lot. I hope they say the same thing when I'm sixty."

"How old are you?"

He loved this question. "Well, I'm going to be forty-seven." He let the answer hang in the air and watched her expression turn to confusion, then added, "Eventually."

She laughed. "Me too, smarty pants."

"I'm thirty-five."

"You're ahead of me by six years. Are you from South Carolina?"

"Nope. I grew up here, in Perry County," he added the location with a country drawl.

"I never would have guessed. Your English is way too sophisticated."

"I know, right? It's my private school and Christian university education. My vocabulary is expansive," but he said the word *expansive* so it sounded more like a country boy saying *expensive*.

She caught the double entendre and snorted. "Stop."

The chit chat continued. His haircut had never taken this long, and he did not mind. She removed his apron and spilled the pile of hair onto the floor.

"I'm almost done. Why don't we shampoo your hair and get rid of all the clippings."

He loved that idea. No matter how well a stylist would use a blow dryer and towel, he would inevitably run his hands through his hair and still find bits clinging to his fingers. He did not want to have to go home and take a shower just to rinse his head.

He followed Holly to the back of the salon where the chairs reclined against wash bowls. His eyes could not help but take in her back side. She was striking from the front and alluring from the rear.

"Get comfortable," Holly invited.

Sitting back into the soft chair, he rested his neck against the basin. Sounds of a faucet turning and water filling the bowl occupied his mind.

"This tea tree oil is great," Holly observed. She put her fingers in front of his nose. "That will wake you up and relax you all at the same time."

"Mmm," was all Kevin could muster. He enjoyed the smells, the sensations and the comfort. He was being pampered. That was rare.

Holly bathed his head with the shampoo and massaged his temples. Again, she took her time. Her long fingers combed his scalp, and she rinsed him clean with hot water. She grabbed a towel and dried his head.

"Back to the chair. Let's put a little product in your hair so you're ready for the rest of the day."

Back to the chair he went, this time ahead of her. He sat in the chair full of thoughts.

She looked at his face. "Are you happy?"

He stared back at her as time seemed to pause. A thousand thoughts hit his brain simultaneously. He had never been asked that question. Occasionally, he was asked if he was okay. He always responded, "I'm fine." No one had ever asked, "Are you happy?"

His eyes welled with tears. Was he happy?

He thought about the rapes that wrecked his childhood and wracked his mind with guilt.

He thought about the hard years of ministry and the families who had left even after he had given them so much love and support.

He had officiated over thirty funerals in his tenure at Glenford, a few of them tragic.

He met weekly with Vic for prayer in his auto repair shop. Vic's daughter, Stephanie, just twenty years old, died in her sleep while having a seizure.

Chuck's older brother, Robbie, whom Kevin had known his whole life, was diagnosed with a brain tumor at the age of thirty-three. The doctor was wrong. Robbie had a brain abscess. Within two weeks his brain was destroyed. Kevin sat with Robbie's parents and the doctor and helped them make the decision to remove Robbie from life support. Sam attended that funeral. That had been a rough few weeks.

He had mentored Jack for several years. In the fall of 2011, Jack moved his family to a property in Logan, planning to build his dream house. He had a massive heart attack moving the last load from his truck and died at age forty-eight.

His buddy Jeff was also dead now. He had passed in January. Kevin preached at his funeral and sang, It Is Well with My Soul. But Kevin's own soul was not well.

Agnes had yelled at him during the holidays over changes he had made at the old home church of their childhood. His family believed he was compromising, and they had issues with Tiffany.

The constant triggers between him and his wife wounded him repeatedly.

Kevin was not happy.

All of those memories collided in an instant. He looked up at the mirror into her soft face and said, "I'm not allowed to be happy."

Her rebuttal was short and snappy, "I disagree. You deserve to be happy."

She applied thickening paste to her fingers and touched his hair at the forehead. She spiked the short hairs as best she could. He looked good. Kevin rarely allowed himself to think that, but he really looked great. His thin face was tan, and his arms were thick against the short sleeves of his royal blue polo.

"You look too handsome to be a pastor. You're ready for one of those fitness magazine covers." She patted his arm. "We're done for today, but I expect to see you back in a few weeks." She went to the register, and he followed. Taking a business card from the desk, she wrote her phone number on it. "Text me when you're ready for your next appointment, and we'll make sure I am here."

"Perfect." He smiled at her, pulled out his wallet, paid and tipped her. "Best haircut I've ever had."

"I'm the best at what I do," she replied with a wink. Kevin agreed.

He did not text her for a couple of weeks. He waited until he needed a haircut. He was still unsure how much of Holly's demeanor was her professional persona and how much was her personal interest in him. Time would tell.

And time did.

A couple of weeks later, he texted her. They set his hair appointment. With each haircut, their stories unfolded to each other. He felt comfortable sharing his childhood trauma. She, in turn, talked about the domestic abuse she had survived. His haircuts were in the morning when few customers were around. After a few months, Holly was ready for more.

"Can we meet for coffee sometime when I am not working? I just love talking to you, and we have these short conversations, and I want some time when we're not interrupted."

Kevin knew he was in dangerous territory. He should keep this relationship professional. To his credit, he had talked to her openly about spiritual truth. But the more he cared about her spiritually, the more he cared about her emotionally, too. She had her own wounds and scars. They were both hurting and both looking for someone to see them in their pain. They found solace in each other.

In those months, ministry life and marriage life had devolved. Kevin was beyond frustrated. He was hopeless. With Tiffany, he had decided they would not stay at Glenford much longer. Unsure of next steps, he had spent time with a mentor, a pastor in Columbus named Eric.

On this Tuesday, as he stepped out of the shower and wrapped himself in a large, white towel, he would be going to Eric's church for a conference. And afterward, he would meet Holly at a mall on the north side. They would get coffee and finally have uninterrupted time to talk.

He was happy now, at least at times. An unexpected text from Holly would flood his brain with endorphins. She truly liked him. Even though he was a mess, she saw the good in him, and she wanted time with him.

He told no one. He knew that the relationship was borderline inappropriate. He didn't care. This was between him and her. No one else needed to know. No one else deserved to know. They didn't care about him anyway, not like she did.

With butterflies in his stomach, he finished his hygiene routine, hung up his towel, turned off the light and slipped out of the bathroom. To the walk-in closet he stepped quietly, a routine he had observed thousands of times so as not to disturb Tiffany. He slipped inside, found his clothes and dressed in the darkness.

When he exited the bedroom, he felt relief, as always. He had not disturbed his wife.

He crossed the great room with its open floor plan of dining room, kitchen and living room and ducked into the small hallway at the opposite side. Three boys were sleeping on this end of the house. He woke them and jumpstarted their preparation for the day. Then he went to the kitchen to prepare breakfast. As he cracked eggs and poured juice and set cereal on the table, he thought about the possibility of meeting Holly. Maybe she would not show up. He wouldn't worry about it. If it happened, great, and if not, no worries. He was used to disappointment.

The boys stumbled into the dining room in varying states of readiness. Sitting at the table, they devoured food. Kevin loved them. They were his little minis, each in a different way. Together, they had a little prayer for the day. Then came the final push to get in the minivan with all their lunches and backpacks.

The boys attended the same Christian school that Kevin had attended. The twenty-minute drive was generally quiet in the morning. Kevin would play a Piano Guys album. Sometimes, a little discussion would erupt. Occasionally, Kevin would instigate some chatter or laughter. Many times, they simply stared out the window at the passing Ohio countryside.

He dropped them off with hugs and kisses and headed to Columbus.

Growing up as an only son, Kevin had missed out on the camaraderie of a brother. Over the years, he developed friendships with church kids and classmates, but none of those relationships had stuck past high school. As a pastor, he had bonded with a small group of peers. They met monthly and had great conversations. Those men would be at this conference. They were the main reason he was attending.

In truth, his mind was largely foggy these days. He never considered himself to be depressed, but he would understand later that he was in the throes of deep depression. His sleep had been disrupted for months now. He rarely slept through the night. Often, he would awake at two A.M. and go to the living room to distract himself from foreboding thoughts. At times, he was able to work, to pray, to prepare sermons and to be productive. Sometimes, he sat in the darkness with no will to do anything. Tears were shed over some of the heartache he felt, particularly when Jeff passed. Tiffany never asked about his insomnia. She never joined him in the living room. She only reacted if anything he did interfered with her own repose. Always, he was alone.

And here he was, alone again, behind the wheel of his deep blue Oldsmobile Silhouette, driving to Columbus.

Calvary Bible Church sits on High Street in Columbus, north of downtown. Near the Park of Roses, the stone building has a prominent position in Clintonville. Kevin pulled into the parking lot behind the building. His pastoral buddy, Brad, part of his peer group, was just getting out of his car.

Kevin lowered a window. "Hey, Brad, did you bring donuts?"

"No. You don't need the calories. Can you believe Eric isn't providing valet parking for this event? So much for servant leadership."

"If there are no donuts and no valet parking, I don't know why I should stay."

"You're here to entertain me."

"I can live with that. Wait for me. I'll walk in with you."

Brad waited. Kevin found an empty space and parked the van. He grabbed his leather satchel and jumped out.

"What a beautiful man purse," Brad kidded him.

Kevin threw the strap over his head and slung the bag across his opposite hip. "This is a messenger bag. You should get one. You're just carrying your Bible and a notebook? I've got a laptop in here, my Bible, a book on spiritual leadership and a journal with a plethora of pens. I'm ready for the day, dude. If this thing gets boring, I can prepare for Sunday."

"I don't think we'll be bored. Eric has a pretty good game plan for this. I was over here yesterday, and he showed me the schedule." Brads' two sons attended the Christian school hosted by Eric's church. Brad also taught some Bible classes.

"You got the inside scoop. Nice. What's for lunch?"

Brad laughed. "Yeah, who cares about the content, as long as the food is great."

"Churches never have good food," Kevin complained. "Some grandmothers got together and made sloppy joes, most likely."

Brad had no retort. They reached the entrance and made their way into the sprawling building. They found their way into the auditorium. Eric was there.

"Hey, guys! So glad you made it, especially you, Stephens. It's a decent drive coming to the big city, right?"

"Totally worth it, if you have donuts," Kevin deadpanned.

"Actually, we are serving the fruit of the Spirit for breakfast," Eric replied.

"Why couldn't it have been the baked goods of the Spirit?" Kevin grimaced.

"Yes, well, let's update that in the next translation," Brad chimed in.

Banter continued as the space filled with attendees.

Eric turned the conversation to the day's agenda. "I really am excited about today. We're going to have some great discussions about missions. I will be surprised if we don't provoke a few arguments. I want to turn some of our outdated thinking on its head."

Brad, Kevin and Eric shared a common passion for reinvigorating the church with fresh thinking.

But the thought reaggravated the burden on Kevin's soul. Some of his church family had not responded well, and he was tired. His attention was not on the presentations or the discussions. He participated halfheartedly, at best. At one point, he dialed Brad's phone as a prank. Sure enough, his friend had forgotten to silence his phone and embarrassedly groped for the device in his pocket. When he saw that the missed call was from Kevin, he laughed so hard, he walked out.

During the lunch break, Eric and Kevin found a few minutes to connect.

"How are you doing?" Eric asked the question with genuine compassion. He knew a good bit of the struggle Kevin was enduring. Kevin had even disclosed his trauma to Eric.

"I'm exhausted. I don't think I can do this anymore."

Eric placed a hand on Kevin's shoulder and looked into his eyes.

"Kevin, it's okay to quit."

As Kevin processed those words, he began to sob. No one had ever given him permission to stop, to say no, to quit.

A signature moment from his childhood had occurred in the old Brethren church. He was four years old. Dad and Mom wanted him to sing a song in front of the congregation. Kevin was scared. The thought of getting up in front of the church and singing was frightening. Dad and Mom insisted. Sunday came. He had sung this song a thousand times. Dad waited for the evening service. After a couple of congregational hymns and an offering, Dad put a chair on the platform. Kevin climbed the wooden stairs to the platform. Dad lifted him to stand on the chair, so that he could see over the pulpit. Parishioners nodded in encouragement, but Kevin was overwhelmed. The group of sixty or so people seemed like hundreds. The pianist played the introduction, and he began to sing, timidly. As he completed the first of the three stanzas, tears started to stream from his eyes. His voice trembled even more. He choked back the sobs and continued to sing. At last, he was done. Dad lifted him off the chair, and Kevin walked off the platform with composure. Inwardly, he was humiliated. He had cried in front of everyone. But he survived.

Years later, Dad would tell him, "I was so proud of you. You didn't quit. You just kept singing."

Kevin was taken aback. He did not know quitting was an option. He had never considered the possibility.

Many other similar moments played out through his childhood. In sixth grade, he participated in a Scripture memory contest at the state level. Children from Christian schools all over Ohio had gathered at a large church in Zanesville for the event. Kevin had committed the first thirteen verses of the fourth chapter of Paul's letter to the Philippians to memory. All he had to do was stand on the platform and recite the verses. He practiced many times over until the words came out on autopilot. Then the youth pastor helped him recite the words with expression and feeling.

He was ready. On a Friday morning, as the Ohio winter turned to spring, and the skies wept over the changing of the season, he stood in front of a few hundred adults and peers and began his recitation. Fear gripped his throat and tortured his stomach. Tears again coursed down his cheeks. Through the tears and the embarrassment, he finished the passage. He did not place.

By high school, the stage fright was mostly gone. He won state contests in dramatic declamation, humorous interpretation and preaching. He was not a quitter. He was winning.

But this felt different. This was not a matter of winning or losing. This was ministry. This was about helping or not helping, and he had begun to feel unhelpful. Now was the time to step aside, to allow the church to reset. Now was the time to allow himself to pause, to process and perhaps to pivot.

Eric squeezed Kevin's shoulder. "You don't have to decide today. We'll speak again soon."

Kevin wiped away the tears, steeled himself outwardly and regained a calm demeanor. But on the inside, he was done. The decision was made. And he knew how to burn the bridge so that there was no way back. Quitting would be the only option.

Lunch was not sloppy joe. Panera bread catered the meal. Kevin sat with Brad.

"Jerk," Brad chided with a smile on his face. "My phone is silenced now."

"So glad I could teach you a valuable life lesson. Imagine if you had been the speaker."

"You know, I bet I forget to set my phone on most Sundays. I just assume no one will call because everyone is at church, like me."

"I'll keep that in mind," Kevin assured him. "There may be another lesson in store for you."

"You know," Brad added, "Maybe Eric needs that lesson. I'm good." Brad shifted topics. "You and Tiffany need to come over again before Thanksgiving. Jen is still talking about how much fun we had last time we got together."

"My birthday is this week. You should surprise me with a party."

"Yes, great idea," Brad chuckled. "Help me plan your surprise party."

"Let's work on that during the afternoon session," Kevin offered, mostly joking.

"This afternoon is a panel discussion. It's going to be great."

Brad wasn't wrong. The afternoon passed quickly. By three o'clock, the event was over.

"Thanks for putting this together, Eric."

"You're welcome. We're still on for lunch next Thursday, right?"

"You bet."

"And Kevin, don't even try to catch me with my phone live during a service. I silence mine every single time."

They laughed and parted. Kevin found Brad, and they exited together.

"What day is your birthday?"

"Saturday."

"Happy early birthday, bud. I really appreciate you."

"Thanks, Brad. You're a good friend." Kevin shook his counterpart's hand and gave him a shoulder hug. "I'll see you next week at the Thursday lunch."

Kevin strode to his minivan. He hit the button on the key fob, and the side door slid open. Slipping the strap of his messenger bag over his head, he placed the leather satchel on the floor and hit the button to reverse the process. He opened the driver door and climbed in. And then he allowed himself to open his phone and to check his messages. Holly had texted.

"I'm at the mall, sexy pants. Text me when you're headed this way."

Kevin knew. He was crossing a line. He did not care. He deserved to be loved, to be wanted, to be seen, to be supported. And he had not experienced that in his current circle, not in a way that made a meaningful difference.

Holly had brought something different into his life. She accepted him in a way that was novel to him. Here was an outsider that barely knew him who had already made him feel seen and heard and wanted.

And that had developed organically out of conversations in the shop, a few phone calls and a couple of months of texting. She already understood him better than his own wife of twelve years.

"On my way." He sent the text and pulled out of the parking lot.

Columbus is a large sprawling city of intertwined suburbs. On the north side, Polaris Mall provides an epicenter for shopping, dining and entertainment. Kevin drove north on I-71. He tapped the icon on his phone and connected with Holly.

"I'm about to pull off the exit for the mall," he informed her.

"I parked outside Saks Fifth Avenue. I can't wait to see you."

"I can't wait to see you, and give you a hug," he added.

"Oh, Kevin. I'm going to give you the biggest hug."

His spine tingled.

"See you in a few."

He allowed himself to enjoy the anticipation of seeing Holly. He took every other doubt and fear and shoved it into the same compartment where he held the ongoing loop of his rapes, the image of Dwight in the shower, the guilt of his masturbation, the disappointment of his college disclosure, the pain of his wife's rejections and the darkness of his personal losses. Today was not about the past. He wanted to enjoy the present. And he was hopeful that the future would be different.

When he pulled around to Saks' parking lot, he searched for Holly's black SUV, the one that always sat in the parking lot of the salon. He saw her and pulled into an adjacent space.

The overcast shadow of fall was pierced by the radiance of her presence. Her hair was raven black and styled with curls and layers around her long, thin, beautiful face. She wore a short leather jacket over a deep green sweater. Dark, tight jeans were tucked into short leather boots. He could not take his eyes off of her. He opened his door and stepped onto the pavement.

They did not rush. He closed his door and stepped towards her. They drew close. She opened her arms. He stepped into her hug and drew her close. He absorbed her scents – the smells of perfume, hairspray and makeup filling his nostrils. He was intoxicated. He felt the tightness of her body, and the softness of her bosom. He gave her a quick kiss on the cheek.

"I could get used to this."

She smiled. "I hope so."

They sensed that things might progress too quickly if they didn't do something else, so they clasped hands and headed into the mall. She was slightly taller than him with her heeled suede boots. Her long fingers matched his, and her grip was comfortable. He held the door for her.

"I knew you would be a gentleman," she smiled.

"Sometimes." He winked.

They meandered through the store and into the mall making small talk, chatting about the day. The conversation flowed. As if they had known each other much longer than a few months, they bantered with the effortlessness of a couple married for years.

"I thought we were going to get a coffee and talk," Kevin reminded her.

"This is so much better. Aren't you having fun?"

He nodded. "You have no idea." And he kissed her on the lips. Her lips were softer than he expected, as was her tongue. Their passion was electric. He pulled back, not because he wanted to, but because he was wanting more than what was appropriate for a mall.

"You're about to take my clothes off, aren't you?" She bit her lip, and he melted. He had never been looked at so eagerly.

His eyes were intense. "You have no idea."

Her hand went to his waist and brushed his groin. "I think I do."

Again, they pivoted, avoiding the temptation for the moment.

They sauntered in and out of stores, and then Holly whispered in his ear, "I think we need to talk in my car."

He melted.

She grabbed his arm as they headed back to the anchor store and the parking lot.

"Your arms are so big."

Kevin had never really thought his muscles were that pronounced. The words made him feel good.

They reached the car. Holly hit the unlock button. "Get in the back seat."

He did. And she got in on the opposite side. They kissed. Their lips were interlocked as their hands explored each other.

"Sit back. I want to do something for you."

What transpired over the next few minutes was the most sensual experience of Kevin's life. She was gentle yet aggressive. She was eager and unselfish. She finished him in her mouth and smiled at him as she swallowed.

"You're delicious."

Holly wasn't ready for reciprocation. They talked some more. Then they parted ways with plans to reconnect soon. Kevin got in his vehicle and watched as she pulled out of the lot. Then he followed suit. He could not believe what had just transpired. This was everything he had expected marriage to be and had never been except for one memorable tryst.

He had never understood those erectile dysfunction commercials that portrayed the male as walking on air, until now. He felt like Superman. The drive home was a bliss of reliving the afternoon with Holly. At home, he enjoyed time with his sons and then put them to bed. He did not care that his wife had no interest in intimacy. He went to bed, said goodnight and rolled over on his side. He was content. Tomorrow was going to be a fantastic day.

Chapter Twelve

Epilogue

From full sleep, he bolted to a seated position screaming. Whether other guests of the hotel noticed or complained, he never knew. His wife took note, however. His panic awakened and alarmed her. In twelve years of marriage, she had never experienced him like this. For his part, troubled dreams were nothing new, but this was a night terror. And this was different.

Not every story has a happy ending, and that's especially true for people working through trauma. At every stage in life, there can be new challenges to healing. My story is still a work in progress. I served at Maranatha for ten years with the specter of my rapes ever in my vision. On a few occasions, I reached out for help with my marriage. One of those pastors was a highly respected counselor in our Christian circle. He knew about my childhood trauma. Never did he recommend that I seek professional help. He gave some generic advice to my wife and me that did nothing to resolve our intimacy issues.

We had a wonderful marriage in many ways. Three sons were born to us. Healthy, smart and funny, they brought immense joy to our lives. Our friendship was firm. We were good roommates and teammates, for the most part. Occasionally, my wife would complain to me that she wished she had never gotten married, had children or involved herself in ministry. Those grievances shook me to my core. This must be why our romantic life was barren. Everything was my fault.

Still, I put effort into our relationship. Birthdays, Christmases and Valentine's Days were observed with loving gestures, thoughtful gifts and endearing words. And more importantly, ordinary days were celebrated with flowers, random gifts, sweet notes and acts of kindness. Our family motto was, "Make Mom's life easy." She was prioritized in every way possible. We allowed her to sleep in often. We kept the house clean and participated in all the chores from cooking to cleaning to laundry. She was a good mother in her own way. Her daily habit was to read out loud to the boys. She cared for them with great love and attention. She was also given many respites to recharge – quiet time to read by herself or to go shopping alone. My life revolved around her, the boys and the ministry.

I was not ignored, but I was not wanted. My wife admired me in many ways, as a pastor, father and worker. She liked that I kept the lawn immaculate and landscaped the yard. She appreciated my thoughtfulness in helping with the cooking, cleaning, and laundry. She was happy that I did most of the grocery shopping while the boys were young. But trauma had done its damage, and I craved physical affection and personal validation all while denying that I deserved any love at all.

"You will be loved when you are good enough" was the lie that kept me performing.

This was too much to sustain.

Then I met someone who understood me, a survivor of domestic violence. She created the safe space I needed to fall apart. And I did, to a degree. I was unfaithful to my wife. We had already planned to resign from ministry. I came clean about my affair two days before our final

Sunday. The lying and deceit bothered me deeply, but finally experiencing something akin to unconditional acceptance was exhilarating.

What transpired over the next few months was a travesty of leadership in the Christian circle I had trusted for too long. Rather than helping me with my underlying issues, they ignored my trauma once more. Instead, I was told to cut the person out of my life who truly loved and wanted me to continue a relationship with a wife who had rejected me many times over. I was ready for neither. I was judged harshly as rebellious, incorrigible, selfish and even apostate.

My parents and family were attempting to find the line between unconditional love for me and unquestionable obedience to God. Many people showed me kindness and grace. Few of them were inside the Bob Jones or independent fundamental Baptist circle.

Survival became a greater issue than recovery. During that time, I ignored a lot of loving, helpful advice because I felt like I needed to follow the counsel of my Christian peers. This led to an even darker series of unfortunate events. I allowed my wife to move to Greenville, South Carolina to be near family. I originally planned to stay in Ohio. But without help and without my sons, I yielded to pressure and circumstance and moved to Greenville as well. With few options for housing, I ended up staying with a wealthy family that had the room to accommodate me. I lived with Art and Kathy Parks (not their real names).

We never spoke about my childhood trauma in direct terms. Every day, for roughly five months, I passed the pictures of Sam on the wall by the stairwell. There were even times when I saw Sam, including July 4th of that summer, when his parents invited the two of us to have lunch with them. That would be my last interaction with him as of this writing. I made attempts to get help from pastoral counselors but soon gave up. Their sole focus was my marriage. I was like a linebacker with a broken leg being told to get back in the game, while I truly needed space to heal.

My wife and I were interacting as we shared custody of the boys. Because I did not get help before my kids were born, my choices necessarily affected them greatly. My heart was broken for them. They were troopers. They still are. I love them more than they know.

Reconciliation with my wife was not an option. Between the two of us, the wounds were too deep. She moved on quickly. Asking for a divorce, within fourteen months of my confession, our separation was permanent. In the interim, she met a widower. They married three months after the paperwork was signed.

My life became nomadic. And that is a story best told in a separate volume.

People are complex. Life is not fair. People who do not understand trauma are often unable to help people devastated by trauma. Instead of receiving the help I needed, I was hurt even more.

That is why I share my story. People need to know that trauma survivors need trauma-informed care. You cannot treat a gunshot wound with a Band-Aid. You cannot treat cancer with Tylenol.

I was a deeply wounded soul constantly offered a glass of water and an Aleve. "Get back out there. The pain is temporary. Do the right thing. You got this." And often, such advice was laced with spiritual pablum, "Trust God. He'll take care of you. Just depend on his grace. Keep praying."

At one point before our separation, I remarked to my wife, "I wish I was in the ICU. If I were wrapped in bandages from head to toe, and my legs were in traction, people would treat me much differently."

Wounded souls exist in your community. They look outwardly healthy and strong, in many cases. But internally, they are crushed and quiet and desperate and lonely. Many of them are playing football with broken ankles, dislocated discs and migraine headaches. And when they have the audacity to ask for a reprieve on the sidelines, they are labeled as weak, dysfunctional or selfish.

Extend a lot of grace to people around you. Some of them will not deserve the effort. Evil, unkind, nefarious people exist as do the indolent and self-indulgent. But your acts of kindness will often meet wounded souls like deep shade in searing heat.

To my fellow survivors, you have my deepest respect and my greatest empathy. Offering words like, "Don't give up," and "It'll get better" are unhelpful. You deserve to be accepted where you are, as you are. Yes, I am sure you want healing for yourself more than anyone longs to give. Take the time you need. Find an environment that is safe. Commence your journey as you feel comfortable. Healing will probably be a process and may be a long ordeal. I'm sorry. We both deserve something that life will often offer only with difficulty. I wish you safe spaces on the way: listening friends, compassionate voices, professional help and continual encouragement.

Chapter Thirteen

Dialogue

OBSERVATION: TRAUMA IS OFTEN INFLICTED BY PEOPLE CLOSE TO US.

For all the fuss over "Stranger Danger," many times the perpetrator of trauma is a close friend or family member. RAINN.ORG states that ninety-seven percent of perpetrators are known. Parents should not live with paranoia, however. Being informed and aware is an excellent step towards protecting children. Great communication with family and friends will help ensure that children are not at risk. Know that people with good intentions do not mind accountability. Do not hesitate to say no when you are uncomfortable with individuals who want alone time with your children. Be aware of what grooming looks like. I would suggest that you look for additional resources, and I would offer three suggestions.

Confront

A conversation with caregivers may sound something like this, "I don't think you would ever harm my children, but I've been reading that most abuse happens with family and friends. If I ever suspected an incident of abuse, I would report it to the authorities immediately. If you ever see any signs, please let me know."

Collaborate

Friends and family who have honorable intentions will want to make you and your family comfortable. Technology has made accountability easier in many circumstances. Work together to create boundaries that protect children and provide accountability for adults.

Consult

Resources exist to teach your children about their bodies in ways that are age appropriate. As your children age, have ongoing consultations with them. Make sure they know that they are safe to tell you anything at any time about anyone.

DISCUSSION GUIDE

Challenging Assumptions

1. How does the phrase "Stranger Danger" shape our understanding of risk?

2. Why might it feel more uncomfortable to acknowledge that most harm is committed by someone known to the victim?

3. How can familiarity create blind spots?

4. What emotions arise when considering that perpetrators are often trusted individuals?

5. How can communities remain informed without becoming fearful or suspicious of everyone?

Awareness Without Paranoia

1. What does healthy vigilance look like?

2. How can parents balance trust and accountability?

3. Why is accountability welcomed by people with honorable

intentions?

4. What is the difference between caution and paranoia?

5. How can open communication reduce risk?

Confront: Courageous Conversations

1. Why might proactive conversations with caregivers feel awkward or uncomfortable?

2. What impact could clear expectations have on preventing abuse?

3. How does stating, "If I suspected abuse, I would report it," establish boundaries?

4. Why might transparency act as a deterrent?

5. What prevents people from having these direct conversations?

Collaborate: Shared Responsibility

1. How can families and communities work together to create protective boundaries?

2. In what ways has technology made accountability easier?

3. What practical boundaries can protect children without isolating them?

4. How can adults demonstrate that safety policies protect everyone, not just children?

5. Why is shared responsibility more effective than individual

vigilance?

Consult: Empowering Children

1. Why is age-appropriate education about bodies important?

2. How can ongoing conversations build trust over time?

3. What does it mean to create an environment where children feel safe telling "anything at any time"?

4. How can parents respond in ways that encourage future disclosure?

5. What signs might indicate that a child does not feel safe sharing?

Grooming and Recognition

1. What behaviors might signal grooming?

2. Why is grooming often subtle rather than dramatic?

3. How can communities educate themselves without sensationalizing the issue?

4. What warning signs are frequently overlooked?

5. How can adults hold each other accountable respectfully?

Broader Reflection

1. How does proximity to the perpetrator complicate reporting and disclosure?

2. Why might victims struggle more when the offender is trusted or loved?

3. How can institutions (churches, schools, clubs) implement safeguards that protect children and adults alike?

4. What cultural shifts are necessary to normalize accountability?

Personal and Practical Reflection

1. What conversations about safety did you experience growing up?

2. How might you approach safety conversations differently today?

3. What would make you feel more confident in protecting children in your care?

4. How can we teach children body autonomy without instilling fear?

5. What does a culture of safety look like in your home, church, or community?

6. How can we ensure that prevention efforts are proactive rather than reactive?

Chapter Fourteen

Dialogue

OBSERVATION: STIGMAS REGARDING SUR-VIVORS OFTEN MAKE DISCLOSURE DIFFICULT.

Some assumptions exist that people who have been abused often abuse others. My understanding of the data is this: many abusers have been abused, but most of those who have been abused do not become abusers. Sadly, just one abusive adult can traumatize many children.

Imagine that society held a belief that every victim of a robbery would, in turn, become a thief. What would that mean for reporting crime? Let's go a bit further. You are robbed at gunpoint on the street. Would you tell your family? How might they respond? Would they always treat you with a bit of suspicion? Whom will you rob and when? Imagine living every day surrounded by that paranoia.

I was afraid that I would become a child rapist, too. This led to some reasonable conclusions regarding accountability that many untrau-matized adults would also practice. I was never alone with children in my church. I was always vigilant about how I interacted with everyone but especially minors.

Yet even the healthy actions were a mask for an unhealthy attitude. When my children were born, I was petrified. How would I respond to them? Fortunately, I never struggled with any temptation to do anything inappropriate with my children. But that underlying stress was not helpful to my own mental health. When I finally received some validation that I was not prone to do to others what had been done to me, I experienced deep relief.

Professional therapy can help a survivor sort through what is normal and abnormal in a healthy adult with a healthy mind. A therapist to guide me through the birth and development of my children would have been able to help me with my fears.

DISCUSSION GUIDE

Challenging Harmful Assumptions

1. Why do you think the belief persists that people who were abused are likely to become abusers?

2. How does the distinction—"many abusers were abused, but most abused do not become abusers"—change the conversation?

3. What damage can result from conflating victimhood with future perpetration?

4. How might stigma silence survivors before they ever disclose?

5. What responsibility does society have in correcting inaccurate narratives about survivors?

The Robbery Analogy

1. How does the robbery comparison help illuminate the impact of stigma?

2. If victims of robbery were treated as future thieves, how

might that affect reporting rates?

3. What emotional toll would it take to be viewed with suspicion after being harmed?

4. In what ways does fear of suspicion influence whether someone discloses trauma?

5. How do communities unintentionally reinforce paranoia around survivors?

Internalized Fear and Identity

1. The author feared becoming what was done to him. Why might survivors internalize that fear?

2. How can trauma distort someone's understanding of their own character?

3. What is the psychological cost of constantly questioning one's own intentions?

4. How does internalized stigma differ from external stigma?

5. Why might relief come from professional validation that one is not predisposed to harm others?

Accountability vs. Anxiety

1. The author practiced strict accountability measures. How can healthy safeguards coexist with unhealthy fear?

2. What is the difference between wise precaution and self-condemnation?

3. How can vigilance become a mask for unresolved anxiety?

4. When do protective behaviors serve growth, and when do they signal deeper fear?

5. How can someone evaluate whether their caution is rooted in wisdom or shame?

Parenting and Generational Healing

1. Why might becoming a parent intensify unresolved trauma?

2. How can trauma resurface during major life transitions?

3. What fears might survivors carry into parenthood?

4. How can therapy help survivors navigate milestones like childbirth and early parenting?

5. What does generational healing look like in practice?

The Role of Professional Support

1. Why is professional guidance particularly helpful in addressing intrusive fears?

2. How can therapy distinguish between normal thoughts and trauma-driven distortions?

3. What does it mean to "sort through what is normal and abnormal"?

4. How can accurate information reduce shame?

5. Why might validation from a trained professional carry unique weight?

Broader Reflection

1. How do stigmas shape public policy or institutional responses to survivors?

2. What cultural messages reinforce fear about survivors rather than support?

3. How can communities affirm survivors without minimizing accountability standards?

4. What would change if survivors were consistently viewed as resilient rather than suspect?

Personal Reflection (Use With Care)

1. Have you ever internalized a fear about yourself that later proved unfounded?

2. When have you experienced relief after receiving accurate information or reassurance?

3. How can you respond compassionately if someone discloses fear about their own character?

4. What language can we use to dismantle stigma rather than reinforce it?

5. How can we create spaces where survivors feel trusted rather than scrutinized?

Chapter Fifteen

Dialogue

OBSERVATION: RAPE IS NOT EXCLUSIVE TO SATURDAY NIGHT AT THE CLUB.

Part of sharing my story in this manner is to demonstrate that sexual violence occurs in the mundane. If you were expecting hotel rooms and hot tubs, party drugs and disco music, this story will be disappointing. Of the stories that I have heard, all of them have been simple. No great seduction was required. They were not abducted or held at gunpoint. I am not arguing that those stories do not exist. But many survivors simply trusted predators who then violated their obligation to protect. Survivors were taken advantage of in houses, churches, schools, parks and vehicles. Even when the trauma is disclosed, few events result in lead stories on the nightly news or a dramatic arrest. Books are rare. Movies are rarer. People suffer great trauma on a quiet afternoon in a church building near a small town in middle America.

Sam was confronted but not prosecuted. Only once was I asked if I had considered pressing charges. That suggestion came from my divorce attorney. At that point in my life, I was financially, emotionally and mentally devastated. I could not imagine adding any more drama into my life at that moment. I declined.

All physical evidence was long gone anyway. Other than Sam's confession, I had no proof. At that point, I would have gained no satisfaction from such an action. I was concerned that he be prevented from hurting others, but I had no personal interest in Sam otherwise.

Many survivors decline pressing charges. This is not because the abuse means so little. The exact opposite is true. Legal action is too costly and not just financially. Fighting through the judicial system generally means being re-traumatized, being forced to live through the events repeatedly in the retelling. RAINN.ORG suggests that only two percent of perpetrators are held accountable in court. Imagine putting yourself through the financial, emotional and mental strain of a trial only to watch your abuser walk away with little or no punishment.

DISCUSSION GUIDE
Challenging Cultural Myths

1. The author contrasts cultural stereotypes of sexual violence with "the mundane." What stereotypes about rape are most common in our culture, and where do you think they originate?

2. Why do you think people are more comfortable engaging with stories of abduction or violent assault than stories of betrayal within trusted relationships?

3. How does framing sexual violence as something that happens in "ordinary" settings change the way we think about prevention and protection?

4. What makes the idea of abuse occurring in homes, churches, or schools especially difficult to confront?

Trust, Betrayal, and Power

1. The passage emphasizes that many survivors "simply trusted predators." How does trust function as both a strength and a vulnerability?

2. What obligations do adults and authority figures carry when they are trusted by children or vulnerable individuals?

3. How does abuse within trusted environments complicate a survivor's understanding of safety?

4. In what ways can communities unintentionally protect institutions or reputations rather than victims?

Silence and Public Recognition

1. The author notes that few cases become headline news. Why do some stories gain public attention while others remain private?

2. How might the lack of public acknowledgment contribute to survivors feeling isolated or invalidated?

3. What role do media portrayals (or the absence of them) play in shaping public understanding of sexual violence?

The Decision Not to Prosecute

1. The author declined to press charges. What factors might influence a survivor's decision about legal action?

2. How does the legal system's structure potentially retraumatize survivors?

3. What emotional, financial, or social costs might a survivor

weigh when considering prosecution?

4. How can we support survivors regardless of whether they pursue legal action?

Justice and Accountability

1. The author expresses concern about preventing further harm rather than seeking personal revenge. How do you distinguish between justice, accountability, and revenge?

2. If only a small percentage of perpetrators are held accountable in court, what does that suggest about systemic barriers?

3. What alternative forms of accountability (if any) might exist outside the courtroom?

4. How should communities respond when legal accountability is not pursued or achieved?

Personal and Community Reflection

1. How does this passage challenge your previous assumptions about how and where sexual violence occurs?

2. What emotions surfaced for you while reading this section?

3. How can communities — especially faith communities — create safer environments without falling into fear or denial?

4. What practical steps can individuals take to be more informed, attentive, and supportive of survivors?

5. How can we shift cultural conversations so survivors are believed without requiring sensational circumstances?

For Survivor-Centered Spaces (Use With Care)

1. If you feel comfortable sharing, have you ever felt pressure to respond to trauma in a particular way (legally, emotionally, socially)?

2. What does "survival" look like in situations where justice feels unattainable?

3. How can we honor the complexity of survivor choices without imposing expectations?

Chapter Sixteen

Dialogue

OBSERVATION: LITTLE "t" TRAUMAS CAN BE EX-ACERBATED BY TRAUMA WITH A CAPITAL "T."

Many kids that go to camp experience homesickness. I was not the only kid crying in my cabin and wanting to go home. The odds are likely that I was the only one suffering from PTSD because of rape. So often, people fall into the trap of addressing surface issues without asking questions to discover the source. I learned how to mask my symptoms. I had to survive. That did nothing to heal my trauma. In truth, my trauma became worse because its duration was extended. Adults may have appreciated that I became low-maintenance. Few of them had to deal with the ultimate implosion. "Early detection is the best protection." If that is true of cancer, how much more is it true of trauma?

Preaching against sexual sin hits differently with a rape survivor. Speakers unwittingly run the risk of piling additional burdens of great guilt and shame on listeners. Somewhere in the preaching culture of some denominations, hard preaching became synonymous with being a bully in the pulpit. One such speaker damaged my ministry in Glenford. I have low tolerance for such ignorance. From my perspective, hard preaching means speaking the truth about difficult subjects. You can do so with kindness and gentleness. That does not make a preacher weak. It makes him wise. Even difficult conversations can be had with humility, love and compassion.

DISCUSSION GUIDE

Understanding Trauma Layers

1. What do you think the author means by "little 't' trauma" versus "capital 'T' Trauma"? How do these experiences interact?

2. How can a common childhood experience (like homesickness) feel fundamentally different when layered on top of unresolved trauma?

3. Why might trauma survivors become skilled at masking their symptoms?

4. What are the risks when adults or authority figures interpret "low-maintenance" behavior as emotional health?

5. The author writes, "I learned how mask my symptoms. I had to survive. That did nothing to heal my trauma." What is the difference between survival and healing?

6. How might unaddressed trauma intensify over time rather than fade?

7. The passage references early detection in cancer. What might "early detection" look like in the context of trauma?

Masking, Survival, and Implosion

1. Why do you think survivors often learn to manage others' comfort rather than express their own pain?

2. What signs of trauma might be overlooked in children who appear compliant or quiet?

3. How can caregivers, teachers, or church leaders create space for deeper questions rather than addressing only surface behaviors?

4. What might "ultimate implosion" look like in adolescence or adulthood?

Preaching, Shame, and Survivor Impact

1. How might sermons about sexual sin land differently for someone who experienced sexual assault?

2. What assumptions might religious communities make about sexual behavior that unintentionally harm survivors?

3. How can moral teaching unintentionally reinforce shame in those who were victimized?

4. What responsibility do spiritual leaders carry when addressing topics tied to trauma?

Hard Preaching vs. Harmful Preaching

1. The author distinguishes between "hard preaching" and being "a bully in the pulpit." What is the difference?

2. Can truth and gentleness coexist? What might that look like in practice?

3. Why do you think some religious cultures equate intensity or harshness with spiritual strength?

4. How might humility and compassion actually strengthen,

rather than weaken, a difficult message?

5. What impact can one insensitive leader have on an individual's faith, ministry, or sense of calling?

Institutional and Cultural Reflection

1. How can churches or faith communities become more trauma-informed without compromising their theological convictions?

2. What changes could be made in preaching, teaching, or counseling to reduce unintended harm to survivors?

3. How do power dynamics in religious settings complicate conversations about abuse and shame?

4. What does it look like to speak truth about difficult subjects while still protecting the vulnerable in the room?

Personal Reflection (Use With Care)

1. Have you ever experienced a situation where someone addressed your behavior but not the underlying cause? What was that like?

2. When have you seen compassion and conviction held together well?

3. What would have made you feel safer asking for help as a child or young adult?

Chapter Seventeen

Dialogue

OBSERVATION: HUMOR IS OFTEN A COPING **MECHANISM FOR SURVIVORS.**

One of the quirks I love about myself is my ability to defuse tension by making people laugh. Between my gifts of being self-aware and empathic, I seem to be able to tactfully, diplomatically and humorously bring light to the darkest moments. This skill was honed in my own mind for my own survival. Again, not all funny people are survivors and not all survivors are funny people. Many survivors use humor not just as a tool for evading or resolving conflict but also a coping mechanism for avoiding intrusive thoughts or a deflection tool for uncomfortable conversations. Again, that is not exclusive to trauma survivors, but it seems to be a motif.

I am a passionate fan of Arrested Development, first three seasons. I have watched them repeatedly for years. My kids watched them with me, and they are now a staple component of family dialogue. I will sometimes remark, "Arrested Development saved my life." While that is a bit cheeky, that statement is also filled with truth. The clever jokes and hilarious content kept my mind occupied and enabled me to laugh in the darkest moments of my life. Calvin & Hobbes was another source of distraction and humor.

From January of 2013 until June of 2014, I survived the darkest moments of my entire life. When I was alone, dark thoughts overwhelmed me. I was grieving the loss of my marriage, the separation from my sons, the absence of my best friend, the death of my ministry, the sale of my home and the pain of my trauma. I worked landscaping jobs until I took a third-shift position at BMW. That job was extremely detrimental. I rarely slept more than two hours at a time for three months. To say I was miserable does not begin to sketch in the suffering I endured, yet alone paint the scene.

I took a job in Ohio and escaped the Parks' house, Sam's presence and Greenville's triggers. My goal was to make enough money to travel back and forth to my sons as frequently as possible. Life was not that kind. Again, another volume would be necessary to tell that story. But binging Arrested Development gave me enough of a respite from my pain and dark thoughts to regroup for each day. At that point in my life, Scripture was no longer a comfort. My cries for help to God were ignored. Reading the Bible was like trying to redeem an expired coupon. Deliverance did not apply to me. There was no way out but through. God no longer made sense, not that He ever had. I found other coping mechanisms, and laughter prompted by Arrested Development was one of the best.

DISCUSSION GUIDE

Humor as Survival

1. The author describes humor as a skill "honed... for survival." How can humor function as both a strength and a shield?

2. What is the difference between using humor to heal and using humor to hide?

3. Have you ever noticed someone deflecting serious conversation with a joke? What might be happening beneath that surface?

4. Why might humor feel safer than vulnerability for some people?

5. The author notes that not all funny people are survivors and not all survivors are funny. Why is that distinction important?

6. How can humor help manage intrusive thoughts or emotional overwhelm?

7. At what point might a coping mechanism become avoidance rather than relief?

Pop Culture as Refuge

1. The author says, somewhat jokingly, that *Arrested Development* "saved my life." What role can television, books, or art play during seasons of intense suffering?

2. Why might familiar comedy (rewatching the same series repeatedly) feel especially stabilizing during crisis?

3. What does it mean to find comfort in fictional worlds when real life feels unbearable?

4. Can distraction be a healthy coping strategy? When might it become unhealthy?

5. Have you ever had a piece of art, music, or media carry you through a difficult season? What made it powerful?

Exhaustion and Emotional Collapse

1. The passage describes prolonged sleep deprivation and overwhelming loss. How does physical exhaustion affect emotional resilience?

2. The author writes, "To say I was miserable does not begin to sketch the suffering." Why is it sometimes so difficult to articulate the depth of pain?

3. How can cumulative losses (marriage, children, home, vocation, faith) compound one another?

4. What are signs that someone may be surviving rather than truly living?

Faith Crisis and Spiritual Disillusionment

1. The author describes Scripture as feeling like "an expired coupon." What does that metaphor communicate about spiritual disillusionment?

2. How might trauma alter someone's experience of faith or their perception of God?

3. What do you make of the statement, "There was no way out but through"?

4. How can communities respond when someone expresses anger, doubt, or numbness toward God?

5. Is it possible for coping mechanisms (like humor or media) to serve as temporary stand-ins when spiritual comfort feels absent?

Movement, Escape, and Survival

1. The author describes physically relocating to escape painful reminders. How does environment influence healing?

2. What is the difference between escape and necessary distance?

3. When someone says they are "regrouping for each day," what does that suggest about their mental and emotional state?

Identity and Self-Perception

1. The author names humor as a "quirk I love about myself." Why is it important to recognize strengths that were forged in hardship?

2. How can survivors reclaim coping mechanisms as strengths rather than signs of brokenness?

3. What does it look like to integrate survival strategies into a healthier, more whole identity?

Gentle Reflection (Use With Care)

1. When have you used humor to get through something painful?

2. What coping strategies have sustained you in dark seasons?

3. How do you know when you are coping versus when you are healing?

Chapter Eighteen

Dialogue

OBSERVATION: SAFE SPACES ARE WHERE TRANS-FORMATION USUALLY TAKES PLACE.

We know we cannot grow strawberries on the moon. When I was asked, "Why didn't you say something sooner?" My honest response was, "For a lot of reasons." The conditions of a safe space did not exist.

Some of that was within the soil and atmosphere of my own heart and mind. My perceptions as a child were not completely correct. I wrongly believed that my parents would punish me (with a spanking) if I told them. I believed I was no longer a virgin. I believed I was gay. I believed I was going to hell. Those were all inferences on my part, based on leaps of logic from flawed data.

And that was a separate issue. The culture of conservative evangelicalism that shaped my childhood had its own atmospheric issues and barren soil that prevented growth. The preaching I heard growing up regarding sexuality was rarely helpful.

I do not remember any trauma-informed preaching. That does not mean that such a sermon was never delivered. But in my experience, trauma-informed preaching is rare. My own preaching, informed as it was by my own experience, was compassionate, gentle and nurturing. Yet even I could have improved my content and delivery. When speaking about sexuality, one must also give space for the victim. One must remember that not all sexual activity is sin. One must carefully delineate between the harshness of didactic teaching and the reality of narrative. "Do not commit adultery" is a didactic teaching. Falling in love with someone other than your spouse is a narrative. Wisdom is learning how to navigate the two. Now, that comment will open up a cavalcade of criticism from certain readers, and I understand why. However, without condoning adultery, I want you to objectively acknowledge the difference.

DISCUSSION GUIDE

Safety and Growth

1. The author compares healing to growing strawberries — impossible on the moon. What conditions are necessary for emotional or spiritual growth?

2. What makes a space feel safe enough for truth-telling?

3. Why might someone respond to "Why didn't you say something sooner?" with "For a lot of reasons"?

4. How can the absence of safety delay disclosure, even when help is technically available?

5. What are the visible and invisible elements that create a "safe space"?

Internal Barriers

1. The author describes beliefs formed as a child: fear of punishment, confusion about sexuality, fear of hell. How do children construct meaning from incomplete or misunderstood information?

2. How can trauma distort self-perception or spiritual identity?

3. What role does shame play in silencing disclosure?

4. How might incorrect conclusions feel absolutely true to a child?

5. How can adults help children process experiences before false narratives take root?

Cultural and Theological Atmosphere

1. The author describes conservative evangelical culture as having "atmospheric issues and barren soil." What cultural factors can unintentionally stifle vulnerability?

2. How might preaching about sexuality unintentionally harm survivors?

3. What does "trauma-informed preaching" mean to you?

4. Why might trauma-informed teaching be rare in some religious contexts?

5. How can faith communities hold strong convictions while also protecting and acknowledging victims?

Didactic vs. Narrative

1. The author distinguishes between didactic teaching ("Do not commit adultery") and narrative complexity (falling in love outside marriage). Why is that distinction important?

2. How does narrative complexity challenge black-and-white moral frameworks?

3. What happens when moral instruction ignores human experience?

4. Can acknowledging narrative complexity coexist with moral clarity? What would that look like?

5. Why might this distinction provoke strong reactions from some readers?

Leadership and Responsibility

1. The author reflects that even his own preaching could have improved. What does that humility model?

2. What responsibility do leaders carry when addressing topics tied to trauma?

3. How can spiritual leaders create space for victims without compromising their beliefs?

4. What practical steps could churches take to become safer spaces for disclosure?

Transformation and Timing

1. How does safety affect the timing of transformation or healing?

2. Can transformation occur in unsafe environments? Why or why not?

3. What happens to growth when the "soil" is contaminated by fear or shame?

4. How do internal safety (within oneself) and external safety (within community) interact?

Personal Reflection (Use With Care)

1. When have you felt safe enough to share something vulnerable?

2. What conditions helped you speak — or kept you silent?

3. What beliefs did you form in childhood that later required correction?

4. How might you contribute to making your community a safer place for others?

Chapter Nineteen

Dialogue

OBSERVATION: REACTIONS TO TRAUMA VARY. You may assume that traumatized people are easy to identify because they respond with hysteria. That may be the case in some instances. However, my response is typical. Let's be clear, right or wrong responses to trauma do not exist. Victims cannot be expected to fight off the perpetrator or to come forward immediately or to meet your expectations as to what "should have happened." Human beings are complex. When I take personality tests, I get varied results. I can be extrovert or introvert. I am generally even keeled and laid back. However, in the right circumstance, I can be excitable. Making general assumptions can be unhelpful, like, "Didn't your parents know something was wrong?" How could they? Because I was quiet? I could disappear for hours when I was a kid. If only discovery were that simple. I have never blamed my parents for not figuring out the abuse on their own. That would have been as clever an act of detection as was ever accomplished by Sherlock Holmes. Some victims may show extreme changes. Others will not. Either way, detecting abuse can be difficult even if you are aware of and looking for signs.

As much as survivors need grace, so do their loved ones. Making the judgment that someone failed is easy to say. What if some loved one in your circle is currently a victim? How would you know?

DISCUSSION GUIDE

Challenging Expectations

1. What assumptions do people commonly make about how trauma victims "should" respond?

2. Why do we often expect visible distress (such as hysteria or dramatic behavior changes) as proof that something is wrong?

3. How might quietness, calmness, or even humor mask deeper pain?

4. What does it mean to say there are no "right or wrong" responses to trauma?

5. How can expectations about how someone "should have reacted" unintentionally blame the victim?

6. Why might immediate disclosure be unrealistic for many survivors?

Personality and Complexity

1. The author describes having varied personality traits. How might personality influence how trauma manifests?

2. Why is human behavior too complex to reduce to simple formulas or warning signs?

3. How might a child's natural temperament (independent, introverted, imaginative) complicate detection?

    4. How can we hold space for complexity rather than seeking easy explanations?

Detection and Responsibility

    1. Why is it tempting to ask, "Didn't someone notice?" after abuse is revealed?

    2. What makes detecting abuse difficult, even for loving and attentive parents?

    3. How can hindsight create unrealistic expectations about what "should have been obvious"?

    4. What are the risks of oversimplifying abuse detection?

    5. How can we raise awareness without creating paranoia or misplaced blame?

Grace for Survivors and Loved Ones

    1. Why do survivors need grace regarding how they responded to trauma?

    2. Why do loved ones also need grace?

    3. How can judgment—toward survivors or their families—interfere with healing?

    4. What does compassion look like when the full story isn't visible?

Personal and Practical Reflection

    1. If someone in your circle were currently experiencing trauma, how would you realistically know?

2. What signs might you look for—and what signs might you
   miss?

3. When have you misinterpreted someone's behavior because
   you lacked context?

Chapter Twenty

Dialogue

OBSERVATION: SEX IS A POTENTIAL MINEFIELD FOR SURVIVORS.

From addiction to avoidance, trauma survivors may struggle with physical intimacy. My experience was exacerbated by the purity culture of my childhood. A certain irony exists in a world where a boy can observe an adult male fully naked in a shower but cannot hold a young woman's hand on a date. Whether a traumatized person grows up in purity culture or a permissive culture, triggers are likely. Learning to identify those triggers is a key advantage of therapy.

I have been blessed with sexual partners who have been communicative, kind, unselfish and understanding. As I processed my trauma, I became much better at sharing my feelings, exploring my desires and establishing my boundaries.

DISCUSSION GUIDE

Trauma and Intimacy

1. Why might sexual intimacy become complicated or triggering for someone who has experienced trauma?

2. The author mentions responses ranging from addiction to

avoidance. Why can trauma produce such opposite behaviors?

3. How can triggers show up unexpectedly in intimate relationships?

4. What does it mean to describe sex as a "minefield"? What emotions does that metaphor evoke?

5. How might survivors struggle to distinguish between desire, fear, obligation, and shame?

Cultural Influence

1. How might purity culture shape a survivor's understanding of their body, sexuality, or worth?

2. The author points out an irony in his upbringing. What contradictions in cultural messaging about sex have you observed?

3. How can both restrictive and permissive sexual cultures create confusion or triggers?

4. In what ways can religious or cultural teachings unintentionally compound trauma?

5. How can communities address sexuality with nuance rather than fear or shame?

Therapy and Self-Awareness

1. Why is identifying triggers such an important step in healing?

2. How does therapy provide tools that informal support sys-

tems may not?

3. What is the difference between reacting to intimacy from trauma and responding from self-awareness?

4. How can someone begin to recognize patterns in their relational behavior?

Communication and Partnership

1. The author highlights partners who were communicative, kind, and understanding. Why are those qualities especially vital in relationships involving trauma?

2. How can partners create emotional and physical safety without becoming overprotective?

3. What does healthy boundary-setting look like in intimate relationships?

4. How can vulnerability strengthen intimacy rather than weaken it?

5. What makes conversations about sexual needs and triggers difficult?

6. How can couples normalize discussions about consent, comfort, and pacing?

Growth and Integration

1. The author notes that processing trauma improved his ability to share feelings and explore desires. Why might healing increase relational depth?

2. How can survivors reclaim sexuality as something positive

rather than threatening?

3. What does it look like to integrate past trauma into a healthier present identity?

4. How can healing transform shame into agency?

Broader Reflection

1. How can faith communities discuss sexuality in ways that account for trauma survivors in the room?

2. What role does patience play in rebuilding intimacy after trauma?

3. How can we talk about sexual struggles without moralizing or minimizing them?

4. What does it mean to approach sexuality with both responsibility and compassion?

Chapter Twenty-One

Dialogue

OBSERVATION: CHURCH DOES NOT HAVE ALL OF THE ANSWERS.

I am a former pastor. I studied the Bible intensely for years. I have read the entire Bible through at least 13 times, and I have read many of the books over twenty-five times. When I preached through 1 Peter, I read the short book over fifty times in a matter of months just while doing sermon prep. Much of the content was committed to memory. I do not expect you to be impressed. What I am about to say may be considered controversial by some, but I have done my homework. The Bible and the church do not have all of the answers. Scripture is spiritual. Rightly understood, much solace and wisdom can be found in its pages. Overstating the value of the Bible has caused many Christians to ignore professional therapists. PTSD and triggers are not terms found in any translation I have read, but that does not mean they are not useful terms or real conditions.

Imagine the silliness of a preacher declaring from the pulpit, "Cancer is not real because you cannot find that word in the Bible." Would you trust that man? If a preacher ignored the science of cancer and denied the efficacy of cancer treatments, would you listen to him?

Where issues of physical health are concerned, the church generally offers a mix of advice that includes:

-Pray for healing.

-Allow Biblical truth to comfort you.

-See a physician.

-Follow a treatment plan.

That approach is not considered radical in most denominations. Parishioners are not ex-communicated for trying treatments like chemo and radiation or homeopathic remedies such as juicing. People have freedom to follow their conscience and pursue healing accordingly.

Why then are many pastors reluctant to encourage families to pursue professional help for mental, emotional and psychological issues? Why are the indicators of trauma often labeled as sin? Perhaps this will change as the broader culture becomes more adept at demonstrating the science of trauma. For now, many spiritual leaders cannot make the distinction because they see all invisible wounds as spiritual issues. Again, there is a tremendous paradox at work. Can you see cancer? Sometimes you can see the impact of a tumor or some other physical indication. Often, you can detect nothing. You are relying on doctors and medical equipment to give you accurate information.

Science has demonstrated that trauma has a direct physical influence on the brain. My homesickness was not a lack of trust in God. Yes, in part, it was a normal reaction to being removed from the known and comfortable. But also, it was an indication of trauma. Defaulting to professionals is not an admission that Christianity (or any other religion) does not work. Rather, effective leaders delineate realms of expertise and make recommendations accordingly.

DISCUSSION GUIDE

Faith and Expertise

1. What emotions arise when you hear the statement, "The Bible and the church do not have all of the answers"?

2. How can someone deeply committed to Scripture also acknowledge the need for professional mental health care?

3. What is the difference between spiritual wisdom and clinical expertise?

4. How do you personally distinguish between issues that are primarily spiritual and those that may require professional intervention?

5. Why might some believers feel that seeking therapy signals weak faith?

The Cancer Analogy

1. Why is it easier for many churches to accept medical treatment for physical illness than therapy for mental health?

2. What parallels exist between invisible physical illness and invisible emotional wounds?

3. How does science complement rather than compete with faith in matters of health?

4. What would it look like for churches to treat trauma the same way they treat cancer?

Trauma and Theology

1. Why might trauma symptoms be misinterpreted as sin or spiritual failure?

2. How can spiritual language unintentionally shame someone struggling with PTSD or triggers?

3. What harm can occur when all invisible wounds are labeled as purely spiritual issues?

4. How can theological teaching account for the physical realities of brain science?

5. How does understanding the biological impact of trauma reshape the way we interpret behavior?

Leadership and Responsibility

1. What does it mean for a leader to "delineate realms of expertise"?

2. Why might some pastors hesitate to refer congregants to therapists?

3. What risks arise when leaders speak beyond their training?

4. How can churches build partnerships with mental health professionals?

5. What would healthy collaboration between pastors and therapists look like?

Personal Reflection

1. Have you ever experienced tension between spiritual counsel and professional advice? What was that like?

2. How did your upbringing shape your view of therapy or mental health treatment?

3. When have you seen faith and professional care work well together?

4. What barriers (cultural, theological, generational) might prevent someone from seeking therapy?

Broader Cultural Implications

1. Why do you think conversations about mental health are evolving in many faith communities?

2. How can churches remain biblically grounded while becoming more trauma-informed?

3. What changes would need to occur for therapy to feel as normal as seeing a physician?

4. How can congregations reduce stigma around mental and emotional struggles?

Integration and Balance

1. What does a balanced approach to healing—spiritual, emotional, and physical—look like?

2. How can prayer and professional treatment coexist without diminishing either?

3. What role does humility play in spiritual leadership when addressing complex issues like trauma?

4. In what ways can acknowledging limits actually strengthen faith communities?

Chapter Twenty-Two

Dialogue

OBSERVATION: TRAUMA VICTIMS MAY NOT KNOW HOW TO TALK ABOUT THEIR TRAUMA.

The word *abuse* has a variety of connotations. When I first described my experience to others, I used the word because it felt somewhat safe. I did not have to be explicit. I could allude to my trauma without entirely leaving my comfort zone. After years of therapy and reflection, I now describe my abuse as rape. That is what Sam did to me. He penetrated without consent. That is rape.

Language is important. The correct terms are necessary. In retrospect, I am surprised by how few questions were asked about my trauma. I do not remember anyone asking me for additional details. Everyone was satisfied with the word *abuse*. Generic terms help people avoid more uncomfortable realities. I do not remember when, or even if, anyone ever asked me how many times. No one asked for details. I did not volunteer additional information out of shame and guilt.

By stark contrast, when I had an affair that involved two consenting adults, I was grilled with numerous questions: Who is this person? How did you meet? When did you start having sex? How many times were you intimate? Where did you meet up?

Do you sense the double standard? I do.

Speaking the truth about my trauma has empowered my ability to process. This is not some nameless, vague shame in my life.

I was raped.

I deserve justice. I deserve compassion. I deserve healing. I deserve safety. And I do not depend on other people for those. I am free to give myself that space. I can now create boundaries around my life. I have a much better understanding of myself. I can communicate better with loved ones. Clarity about my trauma empowered my growth into the person I am now. That process is not complete. However, I think I would be much further behind if I had stayed in the relative safety of ambiguity, if I had just continued to be content with the word *abuse.* Perhaps my wife would have had a different perspective if we had used the word *rape* from the beginning. Maybe my counselors would have taken me more seriously and worked harder to be helpful.

If you are a victim struggling with words to describe your trauma, please get professional help to process that in a more specific way. The honesty required to define your trauma is the window that will give light to those who want to help you.

DISCUSSION GUIDE

Language and Power

1. Why might a survivor initially choose a general word like *abuse* instead of a more specific term like *rape*?

2. How can language create emotional distance from painful realities?

3. What changes when someone moves from ambiguity to specificity in describing trauma?

4. Why is naming something accurately potentially both terri-

fying and liberating?

5. How can precise language empower healing?

Silence and Avoidance

1. Why do you think so few questions were asked about the author's trauma?

2. How can generic terms allow communities to avoid uncomfortable details?

3. What responsibility do listeners have when someone discloses trauma?

4. How can shame prevent survivors from volunteering deeper information?

5. What makes asking follow-up questions about trauma difficult?

6. When does silence protect, and when does it perpetuate harm?

The Irony of Scrutiny

1. The author contrasts the minimal response to his rape with intense questioning about a consensual affair. What does this reveal about cultural priorities?

2. Why might sexual behavior provoke more interrogation than sexual violence?

3. What ironies stand out to you in this comparison?

Identity and Self-Compassion

1. The author declares: "I was raped. I deserve justice. I deserve compassion. I deserve healing. I deserve safety." Why is self-affirmation important in trauma recovery?

2. How does clarity about one's experience contribute to boundary-setting?

3. What is the relationship between naming trauma and reclaiming personal agency?

4. Why might staying in "the relative safety of ambiguity" delay growth?

5. How does defining trauma reshape self-understanding?

Community and Professional Support

1. How might clearer language influence the way counselors, spouses, or friends respond?

2. Why is professional guidance important when processing complex trauma?

3. What role does specificity play in effective therapy?

4. How can communities create safe space so that survivors feel comfortable with disclosure?

Growth and Ongoing Process

1. The author notes that the process of growth is not complete. Why is healing often gradual rather than instantaneous?

2. What risks accompany moving from vagueness to clarity?

3. How does truth-telling change relationships—with oneself

and others?

4. What might freedom look like for someone who has fully
   named their trauma?

Chapter
Twenty-Three

Dialogue

OBSERVATION: **COPING MECHANISMS PLAY A VITAL ROLE IN SURVIVAL WHILE WORKING TOWARDS HEALING.**

Anything short of suicide is a great alternative. I have no way of knowing how many survivors struggle with suicidal thoughts. My own experience is that I have had those ideas with varying degrees of seriousness over the years. Survival is the first goal.

When a survivor is processing trauma, they should be allowed a wide berth to get through the suffering. Yes, we want loved ones to make healthy choices. But until you have walked a mile in those shoes, you have no idea what they are experiencing.

Humor has already been mentioned and given appropriate space. Laughter may not be the best medicine, but it may be close. Whether that feels comfortable or uncomfortable for a survivor varies by the individual. As a supporter of a survivor, proceed with caution. Some survivors may take offense, and rightfully so, if they feel that the weight of their grief is being treated flippantly.

Sleep may be a double-edged sword. At times, sleep has been a savior. Slipping into the unconscious allows the mind to reset, the body to refresh and the perspective to shift. Other times, sleep has been a true nightmare. Somniphobia is the fear of falling asleep. When you have experienced night terrors and disturbing dreams, you may have anxiety about nighttime and sleep. Being triggered by a nightmare causes some to wake in a state of panic that seems to negate any positive benefits. Therapy was helpful to me in reducing the occurrences of night terrors and shortening the length of my trigger cycle.

For a long time, my trigger cycle lasted roughly forty-eight hours, meaning that I normally needed two days to get through the negative feelings. EMDR therapy helped immensely.

Be patient with yourself if you are struggling with sleep. Do not judge yourself too hard for sleeping too much. Yes, you have to find that balance between responsibilities and rest. However, if you had a physical condition, you would allow yourself to rest in order to recover. Perhaps your brain needs the same consideration.

By the same token, if you struggle with insomnia and somniphobia, allow yourself a lot of grace. Seek professional help. You are not alone. Others have worked through the same distress.

Music can be a miracle drug. Certain songs make me dance even when I am in tears. Others carry me into darkness on the sunniest day. Moods can be altered or intensified, as appropriate. Building a playlist or two or seven for working through different emotional states may be helpful. I have one huge playlist, and I skip through until I find the song that hits the spot, whether it's the heart, the hips or both.

Working out and exercise make a difference. I strongly believe that my body enabled me to survive 2013. Had I not been in great physical condition, I may have suffered a stroke or heart attack. Routines of many kinds can be valuable in navigating difficult times. Nurturing your health with exercise and a good diet has multiple benefits.

Escapism is okay, too. I started buying lottery tickets when I had nothing. I knew the odds were beyond exceptional that I would ever win. But the thought of winning gave me hope. I used those tickets as a baseline for my mental health. If I could daydream about what I would do with a jackpot, I still had hope. Some days, I could not dream at all. I knew I was in a dark place. Hopelessness is the brink of suicide. When I was that low, I was still able to hold myself back from the precipice and find my way back to some small sliver of hope. When I could daydream again, I knew the worst was past.

Numerous activities can be labeled as coping mechanisms from the unhealthy extremes of recreational drugs to the more acceptable range of shopping addiction. Helping survivors identify those behaviors as coping tools may help them turn to healthier activities on the spectrum. Maybe not. Some interests that seem to be on the healthy side can stem from unhealthy attitudes. My obsession with working out does not always come from the positive side of prioritizing my health. Many times I am punishing myself for food choices or hoping I can become attractive to the opposite sex. Again, whether you are a trauma survivor or not, humans are complex and getting to the *why* of your choices may be a helpful exercise. However, for trauma survivors, overall healing may be affected by ignoring the underlying reasons for certain behaviors, both healthy and unhealthy.

When you assess your personal coping strategies, you may find that your choices are complicating progress and healing. Give yourself the space to work toward healthier choices, but also, anything short of suicide is a win.

DISCUSSION GUIDE

Survival and Perspective

1. The author writes, "Anything short of suicide is a great alternative." What does that statement communicate about the seriousness of survival?

2. How does shifting the goal from "surviving" to "thriving" change how we evaluate coping strategies?

3. Why might survival need to be the first priority before healing?

4. How can judgment from others complicate a survivor's coping process?

5. What does it mean to give someone a "wide berth" while they are suffering?

Ideation and Hope

1. Why is it important to acknowledge that suicidal thoughts can exist on a spectrum?

2. How can small indicators of hope (like daydreaming about the future) serve as meaningful benchmarks?

3. The author used lottery tickets as a measure of hope. What do you think about that strategy?

4. How can someone recognize when they are nearing an emotional "precipice"?

5. What are practical ways to hold onto even a "small sliver of hope"?

Sleep and the Body

1. How can sleep be both restorative and terrifying for trauma survivors?

2. Why might nightmares and night terrors create anxiety about going to bed?

3. How does physical exhaustion affect emotional resilience?

4. The author suggests treating brain trauma like a physical condition. How does that reframe rest and recovery?

5. What does it look like to balance self-compassion with responsibility?

Therapy and Tools

1. How can therapy shorten or interrupt a "trigger cycle"?

2. What does it mean to measure progress in smaller increments (e.g., from 48 hours of distress to something shorter)?

3. Why might professional support feel essential during certain seasons?

4. How can someone determine when they need more structured help?

Music and Emotional Regulation

1. How can music function as emotional medicine?

2. Why might certain songs help process grief while others deepen it?

3. What role does intentional playlist-building play in emotional self-awareness?

4. How can creative outlets support mental health?

Exercise, Routine, and Physical Health

1. How does physical movement influence mental health?

2. Why might routines provide stability during chaotic seasons?

3. How can caring for the body indirectly support emotional survival?

4. What small daily practices have you seen make a significant difference over time?

Escapism and Gradual Growth

1. When is escapism helpful, and when does it become harmful?

2. How can someone assess whether a coping mechanism is sustaining survival or delaying healing?

3. Why is it important to allow space for imperfect coping strategies?

4. How can someone gradually move from survival strategies toward healthier long-term habits?

Self-Compassion and Grace

1. What does it look like to extend grace to yourself during prolonged suffering?

2. Why do people often judge their coping strategies harshly?

3. How can communities support survivors without imposing

unrealistic expectations?

4. What is the difference between coping and healing?

Reflection (Use With Care)

1. What coping strategies have helped you or someone you know endure difficult seasons?

2. How can someone tell when they are moving from crisis stabilization toward recovery?

3. What does hope look like in its smallest form?

4. How can we normalize conversations about survival without glorifying suffering?

5. When is it appropriate to redefine "win" as simply staying alive another day?

Chapter Twenty-Four

Dialogue

OBSERVATION: PROFESSIONAL THERAPY IS ESSENTIAL.

Since resigning as a pastor, I have spent years slowly working through my trauma. Along the way, I have had a few therapists. Due to limited resources and time, I have not always been able to afford professional therapy. But when I have been able to seek help from trained counselors, the results have been noticeable.

As I have shed the stigma of abuse and become more vocal, I have been privileged to hear the stories of other survivors. In some cases, I have been their first disclosure. Recommending professional help has become my first suggestion. If I could pay for therapy for every adult survivor of childhood sexual trauma, I would. And to go a step further, I would help every survivor find the right therapist. Not all professional counselors specialize in childhood trauma. Not every psychologist is the right person for every survivor. Much like finding a good general practitioner for your physical health, connecting with the right therapist for your mental health can take time. Many survivors either never attempt professional help, or they give up because they cannot find the right person for them.

I have been through that search. Wading through pages of internet results, calling numerous offices, filling out several intake forms, and scheduling multiple appointments eventually paid off. When I finally matched up with a good therapist, all the exertion was worth the help. And in other situations, not much effort was necessary.

When I lived in Boise, Idaho, I had a wonderful friend who knew a therapist and introduced me. Paula was an amazing listener and a wise counselor. During the six months I was in Boise, I met with Paula about eleven or twelve times. I paid for the first few visits and then ran out of money. On what I thought would be my last visit, I let Paula know that I would not be able to afford any additional sessions.

"I will happily see you for free," she exclaimed. She owed me nothing. She showed me extraordinary kindness.

I never expected any service for free or even at a discount. Therapists need their fees for the same reason we need our hourly wages. But that touch of grace, that gesture of mercy, meant the world to me. I have long since lost touch with Paula, but I honor the memory of her as a good person and generous soul. She walked me through some difficult decisions and helped me on my journey.

If I could change just one thing in my story (aside from being raped), just one detail, I would have found a therapist right after I disclosed my trauma to my future wife. The potential impact on my marriage, my ministry and my parenting is unknown. I think professional help would have made an enormous difference.

If you are the support system for a survivor, help them get professional assistance. If you have the means, make sure they can afford the sessions. If they get discouraged because their therapist is unhelpful, encourage them to keep trying. Imagine what you would do for that person if they had cancer. Their first dose of chemo was unpleasant. Would you let them quit?

DISCUSSION GUIDE

The Value of Professional Help

1. What stands out to you about the author's conviction that professional therapy is essential?

2. Why might someone delay seeking therapy even when they know they need help?

3. How does lived experience strengthen the author's recommendation of therapy to other survivors?

4. How might therapy differ from informal support from friends, family, or clergy?

Access and Barriers

1. What practical barriers (financial, logistical, cultural) prevent people from accessing therapy?

2. How does limited access to mental health care shape long-term outcomes?

3. Why might some survivors give up after one negative therapy experience?

4. What emotional resilience does it take to keep searching for the "right fit"?

5. How can communities reduce the barriers to professional care?

Finding the Right Therapist

1. Why is finding the right therapist compared to finding a good medical doctor?

2. What qualities make a therapist effective for trauma survivors?

3. How important is specialization (e.g., childhood trauma) in therapy?

4. What might someone do if they feel misunderstood by their therapist?

5. How can persistence in the search for care ultimately pay off?

Grace and Generosity

1. What impact did Paula's generosity have on the author's healing journey?

2. Why might gestures of financial grace carry deep emotional meaning?

3. How can acts of kindness from professionals influence long-term recovery?

4. What does this story suggest about the human element within professional care?

Timing and Regret

1. The author reflects that earlier therapy might have altered his marriage, ministry, and parenting. Why is timing significant in trauma recovery?

2. How do unresolved wounds affect relationships?

3. Why is it common to recognize the need for help only in hindsight?

4. How can someone move forward without becoming trapped in regret?

Support Systems and Responsibility

1. What role should loved ones play in encouraging therapy?

2. How can support systems balance encouragement with respect for autonomy?

3. The author compares therapy to cancer treatment. How does that analogy shift the conversation?

4. Why is mental health sometimes treated as optional while physical health is not?

5. If someone's first experience with therapy is unpleasant, how should supporters respond?

6. What would it look like to treat trauma recovery with the same urgency as physical illness?

Broader Reflection

1. How can churches or faith communities normalize therapy as part of holistic care?

2. What stigma still exists around counseling in your cultural or religious context?

3. How can we help people understand that seeking therapy is not a failure of faith?

4. What would change if professional mental health care were seen as routine rather than exceptional?

Personal Reflection

1. What has shaped your perception of therapy?

2. When have you seen professional help make a noticeable difference in someone's life?

3. How do you decide when an issue requires more than informal support?

4. If someone close to you disclosed trauma, what practical steps could you take to help them access care?

5. What would it take for you to persist in seeking help if your first attempts were discouraging?

Chapter Twenty-Five

Acknowledgements

ACKNOWLEDGEMENTS

This is not a technical document. However, I want to note that I have referenced RAINN.ORG, and I would encourage you to look through their website for additional data. While the book is a product of my experience, mind, personality and style, I took advantage of ChatGPT for help with the open-ended discussion questions, and the results were helpful. Thanks, AI!

I have thought about this section for years as I have worked on different versions of this book. I am ever grateful for incredible people who have poured into my life. Each deserves his or her own paragraph. I am going to risk missing someone dear to me, but I am simply going to list names rather than attempting to write an explanation of each person's effect on my life:

Kristin Strayer, Stephanie Smith along with Dick and Ann, Sharon and Steve – my second family for many years – Shannon Morgan, Matt Pipkin, Roger Shimer, Kathy Malson, Brian Malson, June Goodwin, Almeda Huffaker, Doris Lyon, Thomas Stoeckmann, Tony Gross, Kate Jiggins, my ever-supportive friend group (Adam Huffman, Jon

Corra, Sarah Boysel and Abby Storms), Jennifer Johnson-Kraintz and Alicia Lykins.

Special thanks to Nicole Dowdy, Ryn Wolfe Farmer, Libby Villavicencio, Doug Wright and Katie Huffman for their direct contributions to the book. Katie is a survivor-sister who deserves her own volume. She helped me with the publishing of the book, and saying thank you does not begin to express my appreciation.

I love my sons: Zachary Matthew, Brendon Joel and Christopher Micah. They paid an indirect price for their father's trauma, and I am grateful for the memories we've made before and after the awful year that was 2013. I hope to make many more memories together (some of them good – wink, wink).

I love my parents, Rob and Karen. I love my sisters, Stephanie and Sheila, and their families.